SWINGIN' WITH THE STARS

"THE RAMBLINGS OF AN ITINERANT TROMBONE PLAYER"

by

Stuart Atkins

To Richard
Best Wishes
Stuart Atkins
ENJOY !

SWINGIN' WITH THE STARS

"THE RAMBLINGS OF AN ITINERANT TROMBONE PLAYER"

by

Stuart Atkins

Published by
Mediaworld PR Ltd
Best Books Online

ISBN 978-1-906349-01-1

Printed and bound by CPI Group (UK) Ltd, Croydon, CR0 4YY

Preface

This is a memoir of my life as a professional musician working for, and with, some of the biggest stars in the light entertainment world. I recount many anecdotes and things that happened along the way; some funny and some not so funny.

It starts when I was lucky enough to get into the regimental band of the KOYLI, - even though I was a National Serviceman, normally only regular soldiers could get into army bands – but the pianist in the dance band was getting demobbed and they needed someone to take over and I fitted the bill.

One of my fellow bandsmen was John Barry and I played in his first band. On demob I became a professional musician playing jazz and swing music for a living.

I played with many bands before becoming the trombone player at the then world famous Batley Variety Club where I accompanied some of the biggest stars in the world including Shirley Bassey, Johnny Mathis, Gracie Fields, Tom Jones, Frankie Vaughan, Vera Lynn, Tommy Cooper, Morecambe and Wise and many, many others.

Whilst at Batley I formed my first eighteen piece big band. I then went on to be appointed musical director of the Dorothy Solomon Agency which had among its clients, people such as The Bachelors, Frank Carson, Norman Collier and Lena Zavaroni. I conducted for The Bachelors at the height of their recording career; they had twenty-five hit records, and the work included travelling all over the world, most notably Australia. During the time I was employed by the Solomon office, I also arranged for and conducted large orchestras in Mexico, Japan and Czechoslovakia.

Later on I was to conduct all the Sunday concerts for eleven years at the Blackpool Opera House for Messers Harold Fielding Ltd. and I conducted his production of *Barnum*, starring Michael Crawford for a season at the Manchester Opera House.

Whilst doing all this I was still running the Stuart Atkins Orchestra, playing for dances, touring shows, backing stars such as Al Martino, Freddie Starr and Lennie Bennett, Tony Christie, Vince Hill and summer seasons for the Delfont organization.

In the 80s I became MD for my wife Patti Gold, who had success as a solo artiste on records, radio and TV. As well as club and theatre tours we did work for the services through CSE (Combined Services Entertainments) and worked in Northern Ireland, Gibraltar and most interesting of all, the Falklands.

Most of the 90s were spent cruising for Cunard, Fred Olsen Line and P&O which took us to all four corners of the world.

Whilst I was working with The Bachelors, and through them, I became interested in golf and I started to play during a summer season we did in Paignton in '77, and like a lot of people in showbiz I became an addict. Through golf I have been fortunate to meet a lot of my sporting idols and play the game with them because my wife, who also plays the game, and I were invited to become members of The Celebrity Golf Tour.

The names of musicians in bands and orchestras that I played with may not mean a lot to many readers, but they were, nevertheless, very important to me because these were people with whom I worked, and made music, therefore contributing greatly to my career.

ENJOY!

Foreword

Batley Variety Club in Yorkshire, England, changed the course of many people's lives. On 10th December 1966 The Bachelors laid the foundation stone for this prestigious club, and 16 weeks later we were back there performing. Maurice Gibb of the Bee Gees met and married his wife there. Many famous acts worked there, including Shirley Bassey, Louis Armstrong and Eartha Kitt, all accompanied by a great band of musicians.

Conducting the band was trombone player Stuart Atkins who later came 'on the road' with The Bachelors as their musical director. Many happy years followed during which they toured the world having adventures whilst visiting places such as Bratislava during The Cold War.

I always knew Stuart to be a fine musician with a sound musical background, also a fine golfer (I taught him!). It wasn't until I read his book that I got to know the full background of this nice gentle man. You too can get to know Stuart, so dive in and enjoy the reminiscences of a true Pro Musician.

Con Cluskey (The Bachelors)

Acknowledgements

I have a few people to thank for encouraging me to put down this memoir – I hope you are about to read.

Firstly, Mike North, without whom I would never have started. He has been my mentor throughout this project and has given me invaluable advice and suggestions from the start.

Geoff Lawrence, who told me I should consider writing about my career in the first place, and has been interested in its progress ever since.

Jay Whitham, Brian Dowson, and Terry Speight who, having read rough drafts of the book, made comments and suggestions, many of which I acted upon.

Ian and Alison Mowat for pushing me to "Go for It!" and for their friendship.

And last, but definitely not least, my wife Patti who, whenever I hit a glitch on the computer, was always there to sort it out, because I have no patience and I am totally useless where computers are concerned!

Chapter   Page

Chapter One

Come Follow The Band

These two were men who had been there for most of my life. I counted on them and their influence on me had been immeasurable, now they were gone. I received an e-mail from my friend Ronnie Bottomley, a drummer who has played with me, and for me for many a year, telling me of the death of Billy May, who was eighty-seven years old. This saddened me because, to me, he was the greatest arranger of popular music that ever lived.

The remarkable thing was, the day I picked up this e-mail, I was reading an obituary from the Daily Telegraph of Milt Bernhardt, and by coincidence he and Billy May had died on the same day - 22nd January 2004. This was very significant to me because these two people were probably the greatest influences on my life as a professional musician, although I had been around music from an early age due to the influence of my family who were all musicians of one sort or another.

My liking for Billy May began when I was about sixteen years old. I'd started playing with a dance band in Horbury, West Yorkshire, at a regular Saturday night 'hop' in the Primrose Hall with a band called *The Regent Dance Orchestra*. The line up of the band was piano, bass, drums, one trumpet, one trombone (me) and four saxes (two altos, two tenors).

We used to play the published orchestrations of the day and quite a few of these were tunes written or recorded by Mr May, such as *Pompton Turnpike, Fat Man Boogie, Land Of The Sky Blue Water* etc. In those days Billy was featuring a 'slurping' sax section and wonderfully tight brass figures. One of his hits was an instrumental version of Nat 'King' Cole's *Unforgettable*. This style became very popular because, at the time, I remember *The Squadronairs Orchestra* recorded a 'slurping' version of *Mistakes* which, up until then had been a waltz but it was now a swinging four beat. Later in his career Billy May became one of the greatest arrangers of all time, backing great singers such as Sinatra, Cole, Crosby, Fitzgerald, Damone, Lee, Clooney and many more.

I was always interested in music. My parents had bought me a piano just after the Second World War and I started taking lessons when I was nine years old from my Uncle Harry, he being the eldest of my father's siblings, all of whom either played an instrument or were singers. Uncle Harry conducted the local *Flockton Brass Band* in which my father played bass trombone. I guess it was inevitable that I would play some brass instrument also. My mother was an actress in amateur dramatics and wrote poetry, while her brother and sister were singers in amateur light opera.

I didn't start on the trombone, the first instrument I took home from the band was a soprano cornet, well you can't get further from the trombone than that, it has the smallest mouthpiece in the

2

band. I wasn't very good so I tried the B*b* cornet, although slightly bigger than a soprano, which is pitched in E*b,* it wasn't really suited to my embeture, (that's what the lips are called when placed on a mouthpiece), I was more suited to something larger so I moved on to the trombone.

As my trombone playing progressed I became a little disenchanted with the brass band repertoire. I was becoming more interested in dance music and jazz, much to the chagrin of the family who were all into classical music. There is nothing wrong with classical music, I enjoy it and play it, but being in a village band at that time meant playing at fetes, school feasts, carnivals and on bandstands in parks on a Sunday afternoon and evening, playing what seemed to be endless medleys from Edwardian shows such as *The Arcadians, Maid of the Mountains and Gilbert and Sullivan* selections. Not that there is anything wrong with *Gilbert and Sullivan* either, I actually played Dick Deadeye in *The Pirates of Penzance* while at school – but it wasn't for me. Brass bands now have become much more interesting and provide us with wonderful original music and tremendous instrumentalists.

In 1955 when I did my National Service, I was fortunate to get into the Regimental Band of the Kings Own Yorkshire Light Infantry (KOYLI). You see National Service men didn't get into army bands, only regular soldiers, but I was lucky because the pianist in the dance band was getting demobbed and there was no one else who played piano, so being both a pianist and a trombone player they took me into the band. They did try to persuade me to sign on for a minimum of three years but I would have none of it, knowing that they needed me more than I needed them!

My first weekend of National Service had me playing piano for a dinner in the Sergeants' mess. I guess someone in admin must have seen on my papers that I was a pianist, so that would be how I came to get the job. I hadn't been kitted out with a dress uniform at this point so I was told to wear my civvies.

At this point of my basic training, I was resigned to the fact that I would be going with the rest of the intake to the 1st Battalion which was stationed in Cyprus, but I didn't know that the Regimental Band Sergeant had arrived back in advance of the band, prior to a two year tour of duty in England, and that he was at the dinner at which I was playing. It turned out that part of his remit was to see if he could recruit a pianist to take over from the one who was getting demobbed, so it must have been fate that I was asked to play in the Sergeants' Mess that evening.

A few days later I was told to go see Staff Sergeant Bill Grainger, which I did, and he asked me to play piano for him with a view to me joining the band. I couldn't believe my luck, and when I told him I also played trombone I think that swung it for me. The guy who'd had the job before me didn't play anything other than piano, so when the band was on parade he played cymbals and basic percussion on concerts. When my basic training was over the other lads were shipped off to Cyprus to

Oh to be young again!

face the EOKA terrorists and I, fortunately, joined the regimental band, which I'm sure changed the direction of my life!

One advantage for me was that I was stationed in York and

one of the band members was Barry Prendergast, a trumpet player, whose father owned the local Rialto Theatre. This was the venue where all the touring bands played. At this point I had better tell you the full name of that trumpet player; it was John Barry Prendergast and after demob when he formed his own band he dropped the Prendergast and just used his two Christian names, I think you may have heard of him! Yes? John Barry. You may remember him as the leader of the *John Barry Seven* who went on to achieve even greater fame as a composer of Oscar-winning film music.

In civvie street, I had served my apprenticeship as a tailor and played music as a semi-pro (by the way, I was a good tailor, and still to this day make myself the odd suit now and again!) After two years of nothing but music I was hooked and knew that this was what I wanted to do and make a living out of, something that, up to going in the army had been a hobby.

On joining the band I realized I had a lot to learn. Trombonists in brass bands read treble clef, but in military bands, just like orchestras, they read bass clef, and while I had no problem reading the music, I had to adjust the slide positions to play as a concert pitch instrument as apposed to one in Bb.

In brass bands every instrument, apart from the bass trombone, which was pitched in 'G', is written in treble clef. I understand that in the old days when someone wanted to move from, say flugal horn to euphonium, this meant that even though they were now playing a deeper sounding instrument, they could still read the band parts as they were used to doing. I suppose people played as a hobby and didn't have the benefit of going to music colleges, so this was an easy way of changing instruments and not having to learn to read a different clef.

There were some very good musicians in the band, one of whom was Gordon Beaumont, a trombonist, and he was very helpful to me, another one was Roy Cooper, a corporal, who was a lovely player in the Tommy Dorsey style, which is more of a sweeter sound to the one I prefer, but is nevertheless still very nice. Roy wasn't a very good jazz player, and I remember one of the commercial publications was of a famous Ted Heath number; *Seven Eleven* which featured a few ad lib solos, including one for trombone, and as Roy wasn't comfortable with this, I concocted a 16 bar solo and wrote this out for him, which he used thereafter whenever this number was played. He was a very good reader, and it is often said – in the trade – of such players, "he could read fly shit", and yes, he could! I have remained friends and worked with quite a few of these musicians I met in the army, and even to this day, Roy is often affectionately referred to as 'Corporal Cooper'.

There were a couple of very good clarinet players, Bill Grainger, the band sergeant who auditioned me, and Ralph Beaumont, who, after I was demobbed went on to become a Bandmaster of an Australian army band. Ralph's brother Peter, a drummer, joined the band a few months after me and after his stint in the army he became the drummer with the *BBC Concert Orchestra* and as far as I know he is still doing the job.

I settled in to the band very well and after a few months we were joined by a few musicians from the Green Howards Band, this was because their band was leaving for a tour of duty in Singapore, and in those days all army transfers were by ship, which took months, you see air travel hadn't reached the level it is today. Because these players didn't have very long to do before their demob, they transferred to our band to serve out their time.

The mid fifties was the time of some of the great American Big Bands, and prior to this, there had been a ban on British bands playing in the States, and American bands playing in Great Britain – it was a union thing! However, this ban was lifted and an exchange arrangement was agreed, so that British bands could tour the States in exchange for American bands touring GB.

The first of these exchanges was between the *Ted Heath Orchestra*, which went to the States, and the *Stan Kenton Orchestra*, which came to GB. For me this was manna from heaven, as I was a big fan of the *Kenton* band in general and of his trombone section in particular, which comprised of such luminaries as Bob Burgess, Frank Rossalino, Bill Russo, George Roberts and the aforementioned Milt Bernhardt. Now to my ears Milt had the most perfect tone that a trombone player could possibly have, and this was very evident on the Kenton recording of *Peanut Vendor*, on which he was the soloist. He also played the famous solo on Sinatra's *I've Got You Under My Skin*. Of the others, Burgess was a wonderful section leader; Rossalino was the one who provided the technical fireworks, Russo was also an arranger, and Roberts was in the engine room on bass trombone. This was the section featured in the 1953 band which came to Dublin but had changed slightly when they came to England in '56.

At this time the big bands were playing the pop music of the day. They were all on the juke boxes and were the equivalent of today's super groups. I, and all my band colleagues were playing the popular dance music, along with the military music of course, because we were all interested in the big names of the jazz world.

John Barry was one of the Green Howard's musicians. He played trumpet and, even by his own admission, would say he wasn't the best trumpeter in the world, in fact, he and I played first and second trumpets for the dance band in the NAAFI one

time when none of the regular trumpet players were available, and we struggled, boy how we struggled! At this time he was taking an arranging course by correspondence from Bill Russo, the *Kenton* trombonist, and we used to talk a lot about arranging and composing because we both had a great interest in this.

One evening he assembled a band in the De Grey Rooms in York to try out some of his arrangements and they were excellent. The line up was four rhythm, five trumpets, five trombones, five saxes and two French horns. I was on trombone as was Gordon Beaumont and a guy called Bob Scott, who was a good player, and it was apparent that he was also influenced by Mr Bernhardt! Another person from the Green Howards was Mike Cox, a tenor sax player who also played in this band for JB. It was at this point that I realised Barry's potential.

After demob, Mike was one of the original members of *The John Barry Seven*, along with Dec Myers, whom I had met through Mike when we all used to meet up in The Edinburgh pub opposite the Rialto, prior to the big band shows there. These were great days for all lovers of this kind of music. As well as Dec, I met Eileen, Mike's girlfriend, who later became his wife, at these concerts, and I am glad to say that we are still friends fifty years later. I did play in the *Harry Grey Band* with Dec at the Bradford Mecca ballroom a few years later and then I believe he moved to the Pacific island of Guam, where I understand he ran a restaurant.

The shows at the Rialto were wonderful. As I said earlier, the first of these was the *Kenton Band*, which included many great players such as Lennie Neheus and Bill Perkins in the saxes, trumpeters Al Porcino, Sammy Noto, and Ed Ledy, along with Carl Fontana, Bob Fitzpatrick and Kent Larson in the trombone section with Curtis Counce on bass and Mel Lewis on drums.

After the *Kenton Band* came the fabulous *Count Basie Orchestra*; this was the first time I'd heard *April in Paris* with its now famous 'one more time' coda. Maybe when Frank Sinatra heard it, it probably had the same impact on him, as he used the phrase later on his recording of *Nice and Easy*. Sonny Pain was the drummer with Freddie Green on guitar. These two were probably the reason why the *Basie Band* was regarded as the 'swingin'ist' band around. Cootie Williams, Thad Jones and Joe Newman in the trumpets and Marshall Royal, Frank Foster and Frank Wess in the saxes – all legends! What a band! The vocalist was Joe Williams.

The Gerry Mulligan Quartet featuring valve trombonist Bob Brookmire, who had replaced Chet Baker, followed Basie and after that came *Jazz at the Philharmonic* with its abundance of stars including; Oscar Peterson, Ray Brown, Herb Ellis, Ed Thigpen, Stan Getz, Sonny Stitt, Dizzy Gillespie, Roy Eldridge, Gene Kruper, Lou Levy, Ella Fitzgerald and so many 'Greats', we didn't realise at the time how fortunate we were to see these people, in fact, just remembering them and writing down their names makes me feel very nostalgic.

By reminiscing about all these wonderful shows and artists, you might be thinking, "when did I do anything 'military'?" It might appear that all my time was taken up having a good time, well yes, you could say that, but the actual band work was very enjoyable, rehearsing every day and then being called upon to play for passing out parades, and parading in different towns and cities throughout the region, and concerts and dances to play for. In 1956, my first year, the band played at the gala opening of ITV for the Yorkshire region, which took place in Leeds Town Hall. Now we had all local news coming from Granada TV in Manchester. Later, when YTV came on air in 1968 *Calendar* took over from *Scene at Six Thirty*.

Later in the year we went to Cowley Barracks, Oxford where we rehearsed for three weeks with the other massed Light Infantry bands, before going on to Earls Court to take part in the Royal Tournament. This was quite exciting, we did two performances a day, afternoon and evening, and we were actually billeted above the Earls Court arena along with all the other service personnel who were taking part in the event. Apart from a school trip to the *Festival of Britain* in 1951, this was my first experience of London.

I had only a few more weeks to go before my army career was over and Gordon Beaumont, who had been demobbed nine months before me, rang to tell me about a band he had started playing with in Leeds, and would I like to come over to a rehearsal. This sounded good, so I caught a train one evening and went across to hear the band; I was very impressed; they were all young players and the leader, a young man called Bill Marsden, had just left the *Jack Mann Band* which was resident at the Capitol Ballroom in Leeds.

Bill fancied having a go at band leading himself to try out his arranging skills. As I listened to the music I very much liked the arrangements and the quality of the playing. It so happened that Bill, an alto sax player who also played trombone, asked me if I

10

would like a 'blow', I said yes, borrowed his trombone - I always carried my mouthpiece - and enjoyed it very much. After the rehearsal Bill said that as I was shortly to be demobbed, would I like to join the band, naturally I said yes.

Before I could take up Bill's offer there was a little matter of the army band playing at the White City, London, at the SSAFA Tattoo for about three weeks. This was to be my last 'gig' in the services, and we were part of the massed bands made up of another thirteen besides ours, with all these musicians taking up the whole of the pitch for marching and counter marching. We were billeted for rehearsals in Aldershot and travelled up to London each day. I can still remember the wonderful steak and chips they did in the NAAFI club!

For obvious reasons, the trombones are always on the front rank when marching, thus preventing an epidemic of bruised and bloody necks on any bandsman unfortunate enough to be marching ahead of them. Another 'squaddie', Ted Watson, who played clarinet, was also being demobbed at the same time as me, and just because we were getting excited at the prospect, on the last performance of the tattoo, we swapped instruments on the counter marching. I suppose this is what's known as being 'demob happy'. Amazingly, because there were so many people on the pitch, no one noticed! Don't we do daft things when we're young and stupid?

The finale consisted of the bands playing *The Prelude* to act three of Wagner's *Lohengrin*, this was wonderful to play, because it is so exciting, especially for trombones, and *The Evening Hymn* (*Abide with Me* and *The Last Post*), by contrast, was rather spine tingling. This was conducted by the then famous Wing Commander A. E. Simms, the Musical Director of the Central

11

Band of The Royal Air Force.

On returning to Strensall Barracks the formality of being processed for demob began. I now began to wonder how I would take to life back in civvie street, no more bugle to wake me up in the morning, no more meeting in Betty's Bar, every Wednesday and Friday evenings prior to going on to the De Gray Rooms or the Albany Ballroom, things would have to change, and they did.

Since those days I have kept in touch with a lot of the guys mentioned earlier, both socially and professionally. I haven't seen John Barry for a few years now. After the *JB7* days he went on to write the music scores of many famous films including *Born Free, The Lion in Winter* and most of the James Bond films, but I've followed his career with interest.

I've worked many times with 'Corporal' Cooper and with Coxie who, after leaving the *JB7* became a band leader on the *Mecca* circuit, and after that spent the rest of his working life teaching and lecturing at The Leeds College of Music. He now plays for me whenever I need to put a band together, and he does the odd jazz gig. When he's not doing that he spends his time with the lovely Eileen at his home in Leeds or his apartment in Spain. "*Nice Work If You Can Get It*" – to coin a song title!

Of all the people I met in the army, Michael is probably my oldest (I mean the longest known – not literally) friend along with Archie Hives, who isn't a musician, but he was the pay corporal – it's good to be friends with these people! We have been friends ever since. Archie – who happens to be the uncle of Glen Hoddle, the ex-England football manager – and I, have a great love of sport, and we spend many hours on the phone discussing the state of football and cricket. We are convinced that we could run the

12

England soccer and cricket teams better than anyone else!

So, going back to the beginning when I heard of the passing of Billy May and Milt Bernhardt, it made me realise how mortal we all are and what a great life I've had up to now. So I thought I'd better write down some of these memories and share them with anyone who might be interested. I hope you enjoy the following chapters of '*The Ramblings of an Itinerant Trombone Player*'.

A slim Stuart Atkins, note the Cuban heels!

Chapter Two

Back In Civvy Street

So now I was a civilian again playing with the *Bill Marsden Orchestra* and we were to play at the *Melody Maker* national dance band contest in Leeds. This was a very prestigious national competition which took place annually, sponsored by the *Melody Maker* newspaper. The line up of the band was three rhythm, five saxes, four trumpets, and four trombones, and the three pieces we played were Bill's arrangement of *The Man I Love* for the quickstep, his transcription of Stan Kenton's recording of *Pennies From Heaven* for the foxtrot, and another Kenton recording *The Shadow Waltz*. All great arrangements and beautifully played, which went down a storm with the audience, but we didn't win because the judges thought they were 'too jazzy' to dance to, well maybe they were right, but they were wonderful to play and everyone thought the same.

We used to rehearse in an upstairs room in a pub in Armley, I forget the name, but I remember they had some great stuff on the juke box, including the *Four Freshmen* singing *Charmaine* which featured Bob Flanagan, the lead voice who also played the trombone solo, another Milt sound-a-like! All the *Freshmen* were great instrumentalists.

I don't know what happened to most of these players apart from Gordon Beaumont, who played for my first big band, Jimmy Stead, a tenor player who I introduced to John Barry, and he took over from Dec Myers on Baritone sax with the *JB7*, Dougie Wright was the drummer, who also went with John Barry and Rodney Cass, a trumpet player, but then went on to make his mark as a first class cricketer, keeping wicket for the Yorkshire second eleven, then on to Essex and later to Worcestershire. He was also a left handed opening batsman.

These days Rodney coaches for the MCC, and we still keep in touch with each other – we are both Huddersfield Town supporters – and I'm happy to say he's started playing trumpet again with a rehearsal band in Birmingham, and he's been getting his 'chops' back into shape with a few lessons from big John Saunders, another friend of mine, who's a well known player and teacher in that area. I first met John at Batley Variety Club when he came with Carl Wayne, and I had him playing for me in the pit orchestra at the Bournemouth Pavilion Theatre for *The Bachelors Show* in 1976 - more of that later.

The *Bill Marsden Band* played a lot of gigs at Leeds University in those days and I remember one time, I think it was for a summer ball, when there were about half a dozen bands playing in different halls. Ray Ellington with Marion Ryan, was in one place, Freddie Randall and his band in another and Humphrey Littleton, Acker Bilk and our band somewhere else. These were great days for dance bands.

We had different small groups in the band, a Dixieland section, a modern jazz group and a vocal group, and I was one of the singers. This group was called *The Crescendos* and we modelled ourselves on the *Hi Lo's* and the *Four Freshmen* who were very popular back then with their very advanced harmonies. We had to rehearse each part separately and then put them together. Until we got used to it, it was very difficult at first because some of the parts were only semi tones apart and the tuning had to be spot on or the whole thing sounded out of tune. In fact, even when it was bang on some people would still find it 'out of tune'! It was the close harmonies you know! It was very rewarding when everything came together with matched vibratos and dynamics (that's soft and loud) – along with the rhythmic phrasing, it sounded really good, and it was great fun.

When I left the band the vocal group was booked for a summer season at the Palace Theatre, Blackpool but I didn't do it because we were expected to change the style of singing as it was deemed not commercial enough, because by this time rock-n-roll was starting to become popular, and jazz harmonies weren't the 'in' thing, so I declined.

One evening around this time, I was sitting and having a drink in my local pub when I picked up a newspaper, began reading it and in it was a competition. To win it you had to imagine you were a record producer, and make an LP of six bands and six singers, and you could have anyone you liked, so I filled it in and took the paper – it was the *Daily Express*, which I didn't normally read, - and I sent it off, and guess what – I won! When I received the call informing me of my win I was told lots of people picked good singers and others had picked good bands, but I put the singers and bands most suited to each other together.

My choices were Sinatra with Nelson Riddle, Ella with Louis, Cleo Lane with Johnny Dankworth, Nat 'King' Cole with Billy May, Joe Williams with Basie, and June Christie with Stan 'the man' Kenton. I was somewhat surprised because to me these were the obvious pairings, however I didn't mind, I had won myself two LP's a week for one year, which was a fabulous prize. I remember the first two records I picked were Billy May's *Sorta May* and Kenton's *Sketches on Standards*. I went on to get a wonderful selection of music of every kind you could wish for. I still have them all to this day.

The only downside to the excitement of winning that day, the 6th February 1958, was that two hours after I had been informed of the win, the news came on the radio that the aircraft carrying the Manchester United team had crashed in Munich. That was one hell of 'a pin to burst your bubble'!

Chapter Three

All That Jazz

During my time in the army I had kept in touch with my old friends at the tailoring firm I worked for and I used to call in to see them all occasionally when home on leave. One day when I called, a new girl had started working there and I thought "wow, she's a bit of alright", so I wasted no time with the chat up stakes and we became, as they say today 'an item'. After a few months it became serious, her name was Shirley and within two years of demob we were married. Shirley and I were very happy for a while but unfortunately a musician's life is often very selfish in the pursuit of his or her art. As the music became more important to me, this led to a breakdown in the marriage and we eventually divorced. I was probably more to blame than she was, because as she always said; "he was a tailor when I married him". I have no excuses.

Many things about the marriage were good, none more so than our children Jane and Richard. Unfortunately Jane has just gone through a divorce, but is now carving out a new career as an estate agent and has a new man, Mick, in her life, so she's ok, and our son Richard is happily married to Jeanette and has a stepson,

Kieran and my grandson Liam. I'm glad to say that both my offspring have done all right for themselves, I'm very proud of them and I love them very much. Neither of them have had any ambitions musically – how sensible!

I was married in 1960 and although I was now tailoring again the music continued unabated, not only playing with dance bands but doing a lot of jazz gigs; I was playing Dixieland, Mainstream, and Modern. I was playing somewhere or other about five or six nights a week, jazz clubs or dance halls. Then I met a guy called Eric Mercer, who ran a band in Huddersfield called the *Metronome Dance Orchestra*, and he booked me for a gig, the odd one became a few, then the few became a lot, till I was doing all their work. Vernon Heap, a tenor sax player, was in the band. Vernon and I became very good friends, which we remained until his untimely passing at sixty-two years old. I remember Vernon going with my first wife Shirley and me to see *June Christie* and the *Four Freshmen* with the *Bob Miller Band* at the Free Trade Hall, Manchester on our first wedding anniversary.

I also met Brian Tann while working with the *Metronomes*, and he was also to become one of my long-lasting friends. These were two of the original members of my first eighteen piece band. One of the jazz groups I played with was resident every Tuesday at The Spotted House pub in Bradford. I really enjoyed playing modern jazz as the band consisted of very good players and I believe that I became a better player through working with this band. There is a saying; 'the better the company one keeps, the better one becomes' and I believe this to be true, at least I think it was in my case!

The line up of the band was Ronnie Baron on trumpet, who I

had met in the army; we used to come across each other on massed Light Infantry band gigs as he was in the Durham L.I. and me in the Yorkshire. Joe Markie and Ronnie Varo were on alto and tenor saxes and the rhythm section was Alan McBride, who did most of the arrangements on piano. Jeff Loriman on bass, Dave Bennett on drums and me on trombone. As well as at the 'Spotted', we played at jazz clubs and universities in most of the towns and cities in the North of England. It was a very good band. I also played with Derek Wadsworth, another trombone player; he and I used to play a lot of jazz trombone duets at various clubs. Derek is a fine player and also a very good arranger.

Another of my friends, Robert Hartley, was running a rehearsal band at the Ritz Club in Brighouse, this was a seventeen piece outfit consisting of four rhythm, four trumpets, four trombones, and five saxes. He asked me if I would lead the trombone section, of course I said yes! Robert had been a child prodigy, playing piano with his uncle, the late Ken Mackintosh's band at the Hammersmith Palais, when only fifteen years old. He was slightly older by this time!

Robert had left the *Mackintosh* band to come home to Yorkshire and he was now leading a trio at the *Ritz,* Brighouse – a former cinema which had been turned into a night club. Later on he became musical director at Yorkshire Television, he also became a lecturer at the Leeds College of Music. He now lives in North Wales and does a lot of the music for the children's TV series *The Teletubbies*.

Robert's son, David, is also a very fine musician; he was the featured pianist on the Robbie Williams Albert Hall concert and video. He also works a lot for the Disney Corporation. I took

David to his first football match at Huddersfield Town when he was about eight years old. Bob had no interest in soccer, but he didn't want David to miss out on something that he might enjoy, so knowing that I was a sports 'nut' he asked me if I would take him.

While playing with Robert's rehearsal band I met Barry Thompson, an alto saxophone player, and a very good one at that. Years after our first meeting Barry became the lead alto player with the original *Syd Lawrence Orchestra*. At this time he was playing for the *Harry Grey Band* at the Bradford Mecca Locarno ballroom and he told me they were looking for another trombonist, and would I be interested. I said yes, and Barry told Harry (is that poetry?) and I got a call a little while later, I joined the band on Easter Monday 1964, which, unfortunately, was the day of my father's funeral. He had been with me to the rehearsal where I had been told about the Harry Grey job, and he was as proud as punch of me leading the section in what was a great sounding band. One thing that saddens me is that my dad was only fifty-five years old when he died and didn't live to see any of my later successes. But life goes on!

Along with Barry, Steve DeVine was one of the other sax players, and I still use him on gigs whenever I put out a big band. Eddie Hargreaves was the other trombonist and I learned a lot from him, he was a very good player, I later played with him when I used to do 'deps' (deps, muso slang for deputising, *muso* – more slang meaning musician) at Wakefield Theatre Club. Roy Turner was the drummer - what a player, he swung like the clappers. Prior to turning pro he had won many individual awards, on the *Melody Maker* contests I mentioned earlier, playing vibraphone! On piano was Johnny Harrison who is also another superb arranger, again I used to play with John at Wakefield when he was pianist/ arranger for the *Willie Hurst Band*. The *Harry Grey* gig lasted a couple of years, during which time we were moved from Bradford to open the new Merrion Centre ballroom in Leeds. This was Mecca policy at the time, bands were moved around about every three years.

After a few months at the Merrion Centre ballroom Mecca decided to change all the band line ups, whereas before most of the ballrooms had a conventional big band plus a trio or a quartet, now they changed the line ups to include more singers. That meant the singers taking the place of the saxophones, so the band went from five saxes, three trumpets and two trombones to four singers, four trumpets, one trombone and Harry himself on his plastic alto sax – these were made by a firm called Grafton but they didn't stay fashionable for very long! So with the new line up, the band was transferred to Hull and some of us found ourselves out of a job. I was offered one of the vocal chairs, but I decided not to take it.

One of the highlights of the mid sixties was that the *Kenton Band* came back to Great Britain, and I saw them at the Leeds Odeon. This was the band that featured a four man mellophonium section in addition to the conventional big band line up. The mellophonium was an instrument created by the Conn Instrument Company especially for Stan Kenton. It was a cross between a flugal horn and a French horn. It had a large bell like a French horn but it went straight out in front like a flugal horn, as opposed to being played around the side with the player's right hand in the bell. As the name suggests, it had a very nice mellow sound (or as Duke Ellington would say a 'Mellow Tone').

After leaving the *Harry Grey Band* I started doing freelance gigs again and one of them was back at The Spotted House, I was also playing at a country club in Mirfield called The Marmaville Club. This was with a quartet consisting of piano, bass, drums, and me on trombone. This was quite an unusual line up for a quartet, but I am fortunate to have the ability to play most tunes by ear and in any key.

The pianist was a guy called Bob Weremouth, who was a very good player, he also played accordion, so when he played squeeze box, I went on piano. I also did vocals. During the couple of years I stayed at the Marmaville the odd change in personnel occurred and one of these was the bass player, Jeff Loriman, being replaced by Gordon Clayton, with whom I had played with Harry Grey's band. He was only there for a few months but he came one evening and told us he was leaving to join a new band at what was to be - the new Batley Variety Club!

This was the first I'd heard of the Club which was to change the rest of my life in so many ways!

Chapter Four

Batley - Yorkshire's Las Vegas

The Batley Variety Club opened in March 1967, just sixteen weeks after the foundation stone had been laid by The Bachelors, who were the headline act for the opening week. This was an event that was to change the face of British show business. The variety theatre was dead, the night clubs were small and nothing more than gambling dens, the working men's clubs were dreary and the ballrooms were closing, so with not having many places to work, there was a surfeit of musicians on the market and Batley Variety Club was the first of the big theatre clubs, which were to become popular in the late 60s and throughout the 70s.

The club, which seated 1700 patrons, was the brainchild of James Corrigan, who was a cousin of the Corrigan's who ran the big funfairs in Scarborough. Up to this point James had been running a bingo hall in Batley. After the evening sessions had finished, James, along with some of his staff including Allan Clegg who was to become the manager of the Variety Club, used to go to various night clubs, one being the Kon Tiki in Wakefield, to relax. It was while visiting these clubs that James hit upon the idea of presenting top class acts at affordable prices, just as the supermarkets had started to do with groceries and household goods.

A theatrical agent, Bernard Hinchcliffe, was appointed to book the acts and before the club opened a six-month programme was already in place. The top London agents and managers that Bernard booked the various big stars from were convinced that Mr Corrigan would loose his shirt and catch a cold, but we now know how wrong they all were.

The shows ran from Sunday evening to the following Saturday with a headliner plus a supporting bill of a resident compère, dancers, a speciality act, (which would be a magician or a juggler), a comedian, a male singer if the top of the bill was a female or a girl singer if the top was a male. If a group was topping then we might have a male and female support.

The opening four weeks were topped by, first of all, The Bachelors, who were very big at the time, followed by Kathy Kirby, Val Doonican and then Jayne Mansfield. This was some line up for a town like Batley as these were all 'big names' in those days. The resident band, a quartet, was led by Terry Heath on trumpet with Ken Newton on drums, Gordon Clayton on bass, and one of the best pianists I ever worked with, Tony Cervi.

The club went from strength to strength with big name artistes appearing every week and it wasn't long before some of the big stars who were booked needed a larger band than a quartet to back them. About three months after the opening, Billy Daniels of *That Old Black Magic* fame was booked to appear and he needed an eight-piece band, so I was booked along with two trumpets and two saxes to augment the house band. Unfortunately the sax players and one of the trumpets had only ever played in semi-pro dance bands before and couldn't make the grade, so Benny Paine, Billy Daniels' musical director, decided to just use the quartet, Tony Cervi moving on to organ with Benny on piano.

In the meantime I was doing my freelance work but it wasn't long before Bernard came calling again, this time for Matt Munro, and with players who could 'cut it'. I was on trombone with Gordon Beaumont and the trumpets were Dickie Hawdon, who had just returned home to Leeds after many years with the *Johnny Dankworth Seven* and then the *Dankworth Orchestra*, along with Derek Harper and Ronnie Baron. The saxes included Alan Parkinson, Ronnie Varo and Vernon Heap.

Kenny Clayton, a wonderful pianist, was Matt's MD, who prior to this had been MD for Shirley Bassey. It was very enjoyable playing for Matt at this time, because this was after he had been signed by *Capitol Records* to take over from someone called Sinatra, who had defected to form his own record label; *Reprise*. The arrangements were terrific, done by such legends as Billy May and Gordon Jenkins. I remember one particular arrangement of *Spanish Eyes*, done by Mr May, which had a mariachi type trumpet obligato behind the singer and it was in about six sharps and a series of very black demi-semi quavers – (very difficult!), and Dickie Hawdon – who had to play it – saying "who the f— does he expect to play this?" What a laugh, but he did play it.

During this particular week Matt sang a new song he had just recorded, it was *The Shadow of Your Smile* from the film *The Sand Piper*, he sang it to the accompaniment of just piano played by Kenny. Dave Allen, who was doing some TV work for YTV was in the audience every evening and each show ended up with him joining Matt on stage, it was just like the 'Rat Pack' at the Sands and everyone had a ball. It was a very enjoyable week, after which, the augments became more frequent. It became so that I was being booked about three weeks in every five.

By this time I was making a good living, making the odd suit for people in show business by day and freelance playing by night, not only at Batley but doing tours, broadcasts etc. Then on New Year's Eve 1967, who opened at the club for two weeks? None other than Shirley Bassey and her conductor was Brian Fahay. With beautiful arrangements by Ernie Wilkins and Ralph Burns and played by a good band made up of players from the BBC's *Northern Dance Orchestra* (the NDO) including Fred Kelly, Ernie Watson, Johnny Roadhouse, Roger Fleetwood and others to augment us regulars. It was a great two weeks and packed every night.

Miss Bassey arrived with the reputation of being a bitch, but this couldn't be further from the truth, in fact she was a pussycat, and at the end of the two weeks she threw a party for us all. Of course, I don't doubt that she could have been 'not very nice' if she had been dissatisfied with her backing and things in general, but she was very happy with the whole of her engagement at BVC, so much so that she appeared there on three more sell-out occasions.

The third time Shirley worked at Batley Variety Club her conductor was Arthur Greenslade. At this time she was married to Sergio What-ever-his-name-was, an Italian, and one evening he was in the control box with Keith Davies, the sound and lighting engineer. There happened to be a pint of beer on the sound desk and the orchestra struck the first notes of the act, taking everyone

27

in the box by surprise. Sergio shot up waving his arms around shouting "Oh shit, she's on" and in the panic that ensued he knocked over the pint of beer, causing sparks to fly at every angle and knocking out the PA system. Shirley went on stage and started to sing, but no one could hear her, so she held out the microphone at arm's length, dropped it and walked off.

Someone was despatched to Wakefield Theatre Club to borrow another amplifier and I think the speed record between Batley and Wakefield was broken that evening! In the meantime, Miss B was sitting on the stairs backstage, drinking champagne and saying to everyone in earshot; "Well darlings if they don't hurry up and fix it, I'll be pissed!" When they eventually fixed things, the show started again and she went on stage having changed her dress, saying, "Well, I had to change; you'd seen the other one!"

Chapter Five

The Birth Of A Big Band

Dickie Hawdon had replaced Terry Heath in the house band by now and I carried on occupying the trombone chair whenever it was required. One star I was asked to play for was probably the nicest person ever to grace show business, and the name; Frankie Vaughan.

Frank used to tour with his own band at this time and his trombonist was Alex McInnis who was a very good player and was highly respected on the London recording session scene; this particular week he had a couple of sessions booked down in town, so he asked the guys in the house band if they could recommend a good local player to 'dep' for him for a couple of nights. They said yes, and I was the one.

I went along to meet Alex and watched Frank's show to get the feel of the act before I had to play it. I turned up at Batley Variety Club and it so happened that Frank was doubling this particular week – that means doing a show in one venue then moving on and doing another somewhere else – and the first one was at a club in Greasborough near Rotherham so we were taken there by coach, did the show, and then back to Batley. I really enjoyed the gig, Frank was very encouraging and very good to work for, and Alex and I became good friends and had a mutual respect for each other. A few years later Alex quit the music business and bought a pub, I learned from friends that he has since died. No doubt he'll be up there in the same section as Milt playing for Mr. Kenton or Mr. Basie!

Over the coming years, I did quite a lot of work with Frank and always found him to be one of the most genuine people anyone could wish to meet, he was always interested in what we were doing and always ready to offer advice and encouragement. He took up golf quite late in his life and I played a few rounds with him, and like all newcomers to the game he was very keen to improve. His wife Stella used to be with him on a lot of his gigs and I got to know her very well. He was a true gentleman and a giant of an entertainer.

~*~

It was 1968 and by now the club was very established in a radius of about a hundred miles. Bernard Hinchcliffe pulled off a master stroke, he went to New York and booked Louis Armstrong to appear in July. At this time he was top of the charts with *What a Wonderful World* and this really put Batley Variety Club on the entertainment map countrywide.

Carl Gresham, the clubs PR man arranged for Louis to be met at Leeds/Bradford airport by a young trumpet player, Enrico Tomasso who was about eight years old and was the son of Ernie Tomasso, who had been a clarinet player with Harry Gold and his

Pieces of Eight. This made all the TV news bulletins and was in all the national papers about this international legend coming to play in a little Yorkshire mill town, wow what publicity! I know James Corrigan paid Louis £25,000 for the two weeks and he lost about four grand on the whole deal, but the amount of publicity gained through all the media made it worthwhile. Had it been paid for it would have set him back at least fifty grand.

After that, there were coach parties coming from as far away as Cornwall in the south, and Stirling in the north to see the big name stars who appeared at the club. Batley Variety Club had become, to the theatre club circuit, what the London Palladium was to the theatres – numero uno!

During the two weeks that Louis was at Batley I was on tour with Bobby Vee. We started at the Ba Ba club in Barnsley and progressed around the north-east of England, also in the band were trumpeter Eric Thomas, Larry Ganley on tenor saxophone and Willy Hurst on alto. Willy would later play lead alto on occasions for my band and he became the bandleader at the Wakefield Theatre Club. Towards the end of the tour I got a call from Tony Cervi asking me if I would be interested in doing the BVC gig full time, as Dickie Hawdon was leaving to take up a post at the Leeds College of Music; I said yes. I started the day after Louis finished and the star for that week was Gene Pitney, with Johnny Hacket second top. During the next few years I played for some of the biggest stars in the world.

Vicki Carr, Freda Pain, Roy Orbison, the Drifters, the Stylistics, the Three Degrees and Tony Orlando were some of the international stars who played the club along with such British stars as Lulu, Dusty Springfield, Cilla Black, Clodagh Rogers, Sandy

Shaw, Ronnie Hilton, Harry Worth, Cliff Richard and Bob Monkhouse. Some played one week others did two. Having been open a couple of years, the club started return bookings of some of the acts and one such person was Frankie Vaughan.

He arrived as usual with his band, *The V Men*, and was booked for a three-week stay. On the first visit to BVC Frank's MD was Basil Tate, but now a young man called Roy Moor had taken over and his drummer was Bobby Worth, another good player, he later played with the *Burt Rhodes Orchestra* at the Talk of the Town, London and still does a lot of TV work. The saxophone player was Red Price. Red was very famous, having been in the sax section of the *Ted Heath Band* but was probably more well known to the general public as the featured soloist with *Lord Rockingham's Eleven* on 'Oh Boy' the popular Saturday evening rock-n-roll TV show.

It was the Jewish festival of Hanukkah, and there was always a lot of banter between Frank and James Corrigan, and for a laugh, James borrowed a couple of piglets from a farmer friend of his. During the interval, before Frank was due on stage, James set up a small pen back stage, knocked on the dressing room door and shouted "Because it's Hanukkah Frank, come and see the present I got you." Frank came out to see what his present was and when he saw the piglets he fell about laughing. He was a real good sport was Frank. At the end of this run *The V Men* were disbanding so Red Price stayed on and became a regular member of our band. We were also joined by Peter Ferris an ex Joe Loss trumpet player, so now we were a six piece!

Now that we had a bigger band we didn't need to use as many freelance muso's as before, and we now played a thirty minute band spot at the start of the shows with compère Jerry Brooke singing the odd song. He was joined by a vocal duo; Linda Russell and Bruce, which, when I first heard of them, I thought it was a 'spesh' (speciality) act featuring a dog, but Bruce turned out to be Linda's husband who played guitar! I'm happy to say we became good friends.

We had another resident act, The Deb Set, sisters Rosemary and Patsie and their friend Denise who were dancers and they used to do the link spots between the other acts. After they had been at the club for a while James gave them a chance to do a spot of their own, and I was asked to do their vocal arrangements. This I did and these spots became regular features. Although I didn't know it at the time Patsie was to become my second wife.

The Stuart Atkins Orchestra and The Deb Set
Sheffield City Hall Ballroom 1970

This was a very happy time at the club; we were all pals and made a lot of friends with the patrons. Red Price was a great sax player and I used to enjoy listening to his recollections of the music business He was actually a Scouser although he had been away from Liverpool for a long time. I recall one story he told me about the time he was playing with the *Ted Heath Band* on that first exchange tour of the USA. They were playing a concert in Birmingham, Alabama and the guest artistes were the *Four Freshmen,* June Christie and Nat 'King' Cole. This was the Deep South, and in those days segregation was in place and when Nat came on stage he was attacked by a southern 'Red Neck' which caused a near riot, so Ted Heath immediately got the band to play the national anthem. This took everyone by surprise, and at this point the whole audience stood up and the bouncers were able to arrest the guy and order was restored. Happily things have changed – for the better! I saw a TV documentary on Nat Cole and this incident was mentioned in it.

Red, unfortunately had a drink problem, and I can honestly say he is the only person to have brought tears to my eyes for entirely opposite reasons. On the day Johnny Hodges, the famous Duke Ellington sax player died, Red played *I Got It Bad and That Ain't Good*, which was Hodges big feature number with the *Ellington Band*; it was played so beautifully, I cried. Then on another occasion, we were backing Gracie Fields at the time, he was so drunk he couldn't even get a sound out of his instrument – how very sad that was.

Bernard Hinchcliffe – who by this time had been replaced as agent for the club – was still manager of Linda and Bruce and secured a record deal for Linda, and she was the first person in Britain to record *I'll Never Fall In Love Again*, unfortunately Bobby Gentry had the big hit, but I wrote the 'B' side of Linda's disc, a song called *Don't Say Goodbye.*

Bernard was replaced by the big London agency AMA, which was run by Gordon Mills and the name was later changed to MAM, and became famous for having Tom Jones and Englebert Humperdink, amongst others, on their books.

Jerry Brooke, the compare was known as 'Big Daddy' because he used the song of that name as his signature tune. The Deb Set had now started singing as well as dancing in their spot. One Sunday band call I was rehearsing them in their vocal harmonies when Stuart Damon, the American star of *The Champions*, arrived for rehearsal with his MD Johnny Hawkins. I knew John, as I had worked with him many times before, because he was Cilla Black's regular MD.

The girls were singing a new song I had just written and he asked if they would do some backing vocals for Stuart's act, of course they were delighted, but more importantly, at the end of the week, John offered the girls a recording contract and asked me if his company could publish the song that we were rehearsing when they arrived at the band call, naturally we said yes!

Shortly after this we were all in London recording for John and his co-producer Johnny Worth – yes, *THE* Johnny Worth, who wrote all Adam Faith's big hits – and the girls, as well as making their own disc, did the backing vocals on Stuart Damon's LP which included my song *Suddenly*, the song the girls were doing that day when Stuart and John arrived at Batley

The week at BVC was Stuart Damon's first venture onto the British cabaret circuit, but he had done musical theatre in the States, and when Johnny couldn't do some other dates with Stuart he asked me if I could do them for him; yes I could, and I enjoyed doing them. One of the weeks was at the Wooky Hollow Club in

Liverpool, and this was the first time I met Dave Lynaine and Tom Steer, who were to become very good friends. During this week I did a couple of arrangements for Stuart, one was *My Way* and the other, a new song at the time, by Jim Croce who had just died; it was called *Bad, Bad Leroy Brown*.

By this time I had formed my 'big band', which came about because I had been doing all the arrangements for the club's six piece and wondered if I would be able to arrange for a larger combination. So I did a couple of scores and got all the musicians, whom we called upon when we augmented for certain artistes, to come in one Sunday morning for a 'blow' before the main band call at two o'clock. To my delight, it worked.

The first public performance of the *Stuart Atkins Orchestra* was to play a thirty minute spot in the first half of the show and then back the fabulous Eartha Kitt for her week at the club. She was sensational and not only that, she was a lovely person and very generous with her champagne, which she drank before every show – "very good for the voice dahling"- yes

ABC Yarmouth 1979

I know it's spelt wrongly, but that is how she said it in that sultry voice of hers. She also had the strongest grip I have ever known, it was just like a vice. The 'spesh' act on the show that week had a snake, and she was forever playing with this thing. It made a great prop for publicity pictures and she got some good ones.

A lot of after show parties took place thrown by Betty Corrigan, James' wife, and she didn't need much of an excuse to throw them, usually at the rate of two a month! They'd be attended by the artists, the club staff, a few friends and, as with all things showbiz, a few hangers on. I remember one party when Miss Bassey was there, she spent the whole time talking with the band; she had no time at all for the hangers on.

Chapter Six

Great Arrangements

We had a lot of laughs in those days; I remember when Al Read appeared at the club we spent an hour searching for the 'right sound' for a door knock. Al Read was a well known radio comic and that meant that a lot of his humour relied on certain sounds. So the sound technician ran a two hundred and fifty feet plus mike lead to various parts of the club, to find this particular sound for 'his nibs'. Gents toilet – "knock knock" - NO! Dressing room door – "knock knock" – NO! Beer cellar – "knock knock" – NO! This went on all over the building 'till finally we found the perfect "knock" in the kitchen, and it was on the side of the deep fat fryer, which cooked the scampi and chips, EUREKA! And this meant someone had to hold a microphone near the fryer for about thirty minutes into the act, and to knock on a given cue just for Al Read to shout "come in". What a palaver!

The Deb Set finally had their first record released; this was a song I had written called *People Ask What Love Is* produced by the two Johnnys, Hawkins and Worth. The 'B' side was another of my songs; *There'll Be No More Sad Tomorrows*. At this time we were not convinced that the Deb Set sounded quite right for a recording group (very 60s' wasn't it?), so after a lot of suggestions I came up with Cool Breeze, I don't know why but it just sounded right, so Cool Breeze it was.

When the record company sent out the demo pressings to all the radio and TV stations, agents and producers, I got a call from a well-known agent; Dorothy Solomon, and she asked me about this group Cool Breeze. It appears Dorothy had been listening to the record with one of her acts – The Bachelors – and asked them if they knew who this girl group was. Con Clusky, the lead singer noticed my name as the composer of the songs, so putting two and two together, and knowing that I was at Batley, he wondered if it was the 'Debs' and sure enough he was right. Dorothy asked me if the girls would be interested in a management deal and when I told the girls about this, they were over the moon at the thought of being with such a powerful London agency.

A few days later we were all on our way to London where a deal was done and Cool Breeze became part of a stable of artists which included The Bachelors, Norman Collier, Frank Carson, Karen Young (No.1 with *Nobody's Child*), Freddie Davies and later on, Neil Reed and Lena Zavaroni. Quite a galaxy of names there and the girls went off to pursue a career on the showbiz circuit of clubs and theatres and became very successful.

Meanwhile I carried on playing trombone and arranging for the band at BVC and backing some of the biggest stars in the world. One of which was Johnny Mathis.

Mathis was a superb performer, consummate and charismatic are two words that spring to mind when describing him. Whenever he appeared at the club we always had a rehearsal two days before opening. We'd run through all the charts, (that's more muso slang, for band parts), on the Saturday afternoon with his MD, a gentleman called Roy Rogasin – a brilliant conductor; then Mathis would come in on the Sunday and sing through the programme with the orchestra, which was twenty-eight pieces, made up of the usual big band line up plus French horns, percussion and a string section.

The arrangements were terrific and wonderful to play, done by D'arniel Pursing – I'd never heard of him prior to this but what a great arranger he is. I've heard a lot of him since! I particularly remember the *West Side Story Medley*, it had a beautiful intro played by the trombone section starting with *Maria* going soaring up to a top 'C', and Mr. Rogasin complimented the trombone section and its leader (me) at the end of the first rehearsal. Wow!

When the show opened on the Sunday evening Johnny Mathis came on stage and sang for about twenty-five minutes before he said; "good evening, and now a song by Ivor Novello" and he emphasised the OR in Ivor. The song was *And Her Mother Came Too*. He then continued his programme for another forty-five minutes after which the audience went wild, and before the applause had stopped he was in Corrigan's Roller and half way back to the Queen's Hotel in Leeds. How's that for style!

His programme was exactly the same as his double album LP, *Johnny Mathis Live in Las Vegas;* a Rojohn production, which is a company jointly owned by Mathis and Rogasin, it is well worth a listen! I believe it is now available on CD. Later Roy Rogasin became musical director of the *Cleveland Symphony Orchestra*. What did I say earlier about the company one keeps?!

During this period I was running the *Stuart Atkins Orchestra* and we used to do gigs away from the club from time to time, a lot of this was due to the encouragement I received from James Corrigan's business partner Derek Ford, who was a big band fan. We did a series of dances at Castleford Civic Centre and the ballroom in Sheffield City Hall; we also did concerts at the Carlinghow Club every Tuesday evening. Through these appearances we built up a good reputation and quite a large following.

As time went by Derek provided us with a set of monogrammed music stands along with blue jackets, light grey trousers and matching ties, so now, as well as sounding good we looked good! When Hughie Green did a week at the club Derek fixed us an audition for *Opportunity Knocks*, which we passed with flying colours. I can't say I was very impressed with Mr.Green, I remember being introduced to him; he had the weakest of handshakes and as this was happening he turned to speak to someone else at the same time. I'm sorry, but I have no time for people like that ! We didn't win *Op Knocks* of course but we had some good publicity out of it.

Around this time there was a period at the BVC when Jerry Brooke, the compère, was involved in a car crash. Unfortunately for him he had to have his jaw wired up, and as a consequence he was off work for about six months during which time, as well as playing trombone, I also did the compère's job. This meant I got to sing a little in the band spot, and then I would introduce the first act and dash around back stage and then slip through the wings onto the rostrum and play with the band. At the end of the act I would slip off the stand, put on a cheesy smile and then walk through the wings and say "Ladies and Gentlemen, a big hand for so-and-so", the name of whoever the act might be.

When Stuart Damon was starring, the second top was Jerry Munro, who had just had a hit with the old Gracie Fields song *Sally*, and I remember diving from the bandstand to take him off and I must have had a blackout because instead of saying "Ladies and Gentlemen, a big hand for Jerry Munro" I said, "a big hand for Stuart Damon" and I couldn't find a hole big enough to hide in 'cos the difference in stature couldn't have been greater; Stuart, all six foot two of American 'beefcake' and Jerry, five feet nothing of Geordie weediness! Another memory to smile about.

Speaking of Gracie Fields; what a star! This woman had more charisma in her little finger than twenty current pop idols. During the band call whilst she was rehearsing, one of the security guards came into the club to have a listen – which he often did – and as usual he had his Alsatian dog with him on a short lead. This dog was so nasty it made Hitler seem like the Pope, it was really vicious. As Gracie was moving around the stage she called to the dog "come on then",

"Oh no Miss Fields," said the security man. "He's too dangerous."

But she said "oh it's alright, come on lad." And the dog went up the steps onto the stage where Gracie patted his head and said "lie down" and for the next half hour the dog lay there with his head on his front paws and never moved. That dog was transfixed by this woman and whatever she had, he knew it. The following morning the *Daily Express* carried a picture of the dog looking up at Gracie with the caption '*Gracie tames the beast*'.

When she opened on the Sunday, Gracie closed the first half of the show. This was because Ronnie Dukes and Ricki Lee were the main support act. They were very big at the time, and the management felt that Gracie might struggle to follow them. So they approached Miss Fields, telling her that the show would not finish 'till after midnight and in view of her age – I think she was 74 at the time – maybe it would be better for her to close the first half and let Dukes and Lee close the show.

She answered with "Oh that's alright luv, I'll do whatever you want". So that is what happened. But what happened in the show was somewhat different to what had been anticipated. Gracie closed the first half as planned and brought the house down. The audience wouldn't let her go, they went wild and she eventually got off stage after several curtain calls.

Gracie Fields with The Deb Set

When Dukes and Lee went on after the interval they struggled like mad. So on the Monday, the management again went to Gracie and said "Miss Fields, would you please close the show as we feel it would be better", and the answer came back; "Oh that's all right luv, I'll do whatever you want"! Touché!

That week brought all the 'luvvies' and 'beautiful people' to the club to pay homage to this legend. Among them was Alyn Ainsworth, the TV musical director, Norman Newell, the songwriter and EMI record producer, and David Bell, Head of Light Entertainment at LWT. It was like 'Gay Pride Week!'

The BBC recorded the show for the World Service, and I kept

getting royalty cheques for many years after. Gracie told the Deb Set that if they ever went to Capri they must call and see her. A few years later, as Cool Breeze, we were working on a cruise ship which called at Naples and we went across to the island and called to see her. We were made most welcome and when we arrived she said to her husband "Boris, put the kettle on", and we had tea and biscuits with her, sitting around her swimming pool.

Me and 'our' Gracie

Loads of well-known singers appeared at the club, Vicki Carr being one of them; she had a hit with *It Must Be Him* and she was famous for crying during the performance. Her arrangements were done by Bob Florence of *Mercury Records* who became very well known amongst musician for a series of albums released in the 80s featuring all the top Hollywood studio musicians

Englebert Humperdink came a couple of times and did well, especially with the ladies. The house band never played for Englebert though as he always brought the *Tony Evans Band* with him.

Another nice lady for whom I enjoyed playing was Vera Lynn. Her husband, and manager Harry was with her and I had many interesting conversations with him about the days when he was the lead alto saxophone and clarinet player with Ambrose, the well known pre-war bandleader. They met when Vera, then a very young girl, became the singer with the band, and they were together right up to a few years ago, when sadly Harry passed away.

Vera's week coincided with the time I was doing the compère's job, during Jerry Brooke's absence, and someone told her it was my anniversary; at the time I was married to Shirley, who was in the audience, and Vera invited me to put down the trombone and leave the band rostrum and we danced the *Anniversary Waltz* on stage. A very nice lady. Of course, "there is nothing like a Dame"!

During Tom Jones' engagement his Musical Director, Johnny Spence, had a broken leg and with having a pot on it he had to sit on a tall stool to conduct the orchestra. Johnny was a very good arranger and at the time, Ella Fitzgerald was touring England with 'Jazz at the Phil', the Beatles were at the height of their fame and her record company wanted her to record a Beatles number, she did and Johnny was the arranger; it was a super swinging version of *Can't Buy Me Love*.

The two weeks of Tom Jones were very good and a lot of fun. Quite a few practical jokes went on between Tom and James Corrigan; they were both jokers, but I believe James had the last laugh on Tom. After finishing on the Saturday evening Tom went back to the Queen's Hotel in Leeds. When he went outside on the Sunday morning to go back home to London, he found his Rolls Royce had four flat tyres. I wonder who the culprit was?

Bruce Forsyth was another star who worked with us. Bruce is a great entertainer and very talented. In his show he not only sang and danced and was very funny, he is also a very good pianist and plays very well in the style of Errol Garner. He played *Misty*; I'll forgive him for playing it in 'F', even though it's written in 'E*b*', because he played it so well. His MD that week was Colin Keys. Colin was MD for Des O'Connor on his TV chat show a few years later.

Having mentioned Des, I don't know whether to describe him as a comedian or a singer, like Bruce, he is very versatile, I suppose 'all round entertainers' best describes them both.

Des arrived straight from a summer season in Blackpool, having finished at the ABC Theatre on the Saturday and opening at BVC on the Sunday, and he brought with him some of the musicians who had been working with him at the ABC to augment our band. During one part of his show his road manager brought on stage a supermarket trolley full of 'goodies', packs of biscuits, sweets, etc. which he threw out to the audience – it was like a pantomime. It was a bloody pantomime! However, at the end of the week everyone in the band was given a bottle of whisky – a present from Des – which was very nice of him, but the Deb Set, who had been doing vocal backing for him all week, only got a packet of marshmallows each from the trolley, which didn't go down very well!

Moira Anderson is another lovely lady who worked with us and she was sharing the top of the bill with Reginald Dixon, the famous Blackpool Tower organist.

Reginald closed the first half, playing a large theatre organ brought in especially for the week. I have to say at this point, I hate theatre organs; I don't mind Grand Organs playing classical organ music, but theatre organs, no! I feel that most theatre organists try to play everything too fast and in the end it all finishes up in a big noisy jumble. But apart from that, Reg was a very nice fellow.

For Moira's part, she was a delight to play for and she enjoyed a very good week, not least of all because she had Tony Cervi, our pianist, to accompany her on some of her songs, and as I said earlier, he was one of the best accompanists I have ever known. Sadly, Tony who lived in Bradford, a few years ago died of a heart attack whilst getting dressed to go to a gig.

Because we enjoyed playing for her, at the end of the week we presented Moira with a bouquet, but I have to say she returned the compliment with a bottle of scotch for each of us. For some reason we called her "Matron", I think it was to do with the fact that Red Price was having one of his periodic attacks of gout – brought on by too much lifting of the elbow – and she would gently chastise him in that lovely "Miss Jean Brody" Scottish accent of hers; "Now Red, you mustn't drink too much and you must watch what you eat." We all loved her, and she was known as "Matron" thereafter.

The only downside to that week was that the management insisted that Reginald joined us for the finale, which was *Land of Hope and Glory*. Unfortunately, it sounded as though Moira was singing to the accompaniment of a Sherman tank, everything was so heavy. Having said that (oops, my first cliché), it was a very good week, at the end of which we were introduced to Moira's husband Stuart, a surgeon, who had driven down from Glasgow to take her home.

Chapter Seven

Brass Band Connections

The big band was going from strength to strength and this was the time we were doing the regular Castleford gig. During this period we did *Opportunity Knocks*. Peter Ferris, from the house band, was our lead trumpet player, he being the only one of the Batley Variety Club resident musicians to play regularly in the *Stuart Atkins Orchestra*. We played a number I had written called *Basie's Bounce*, which was a twelve bar blues in the same vain as *One o'clock Jump* and other swing numbers of that type. In hindsight I think maybe it was the wrong choice, but it did give a chance for the various soloists to shine, and all the other bands who had been on the show had played Glen Miller tunes, which I didn't want to do. Of course, you'd expect nothing less from a Kenton fan!

The mention of Stan Kenton reminds me that a lot of the big American bands often played 'one nighters' at Wakefield Theatre Club, and if we had a top of the bill at Batley, such as a self contained group or a star who had brought their own backing, then we, the house band, would finish at the interval. Fortunately for me some of these shows coincided with the Wakefield 'one nighters'. When 'Stan the Man' appeared at Wakefield, Joe 'Mr Piano' Henderson was a support act at Batley and we went to the show together. Other shows I was able to see which coincided with early finishes were the bands of Woody Herman and Buddy Rich, and singers Ella Fitzgerald and Tony Bennett.

From time to time I had some very good players in my band, as I said earlier Peter had been lead trumpet with Joe Loss and his featured number in the *Loss Band* was the version recorded by Maynard Ferguson with the Kenton band of *Hot Canary*, which is beyond the capabilities of many trumpet players as it is in the very high register of the instrument.

One player I am very proud of is Derek Southcott. Derek was brought to my attention by Brian Tann who had met him whilst playing in the orchestra for an amateur musical production. Up to this point Derek had been playing second trombone with the famous *Black Dyke Mills* brass band but he wanted to broaden his musical sights and get into dance and swing music, so I invited him to come along for a 'blow'.

My bass trombonist, Stuart Wilson, was leaving the band shortly so I gave Derek the chance to join us in his place. It wasn't long before I realised that here was a good player who had to be encouraged, it so happened that the guy on lead trombone wasn't very happy with some of the other players, a clash of personalities I guess, so when he left I took Derek on one side, and taught him all I knew about leading a section and how to phrase. I rehearsed the 'bone section separately, and it wasn't long before this section was just as good as the rest of the band.

Derek was quick to grasp the nuances of big band phrasing

and led the section very well. Up to this point he had been a draughtsman in his 'day job' and he came to me about a year later and told me he had been approached by Willey Hurst, the band leader at Wakefield Theatre Club with a view to joining them, and asked what should he do? I said that if he was going to turn pro this was as good an offer as he could get because he would be playing second trombone to Eddie Hargreaves, just as I had and it didn't get any better than that. I'm proud to say that Derek went on to play lead trombone with the BBC's *NDO*, and after that was lead with the *Syd Lawrence Orchestra* for twenty-two years.

I remember once driving up the M1 in the early hours of the morning, after a gig somewhere and Stuart Hall was on Radio Two doing his late night show. Derek's quartet – which was made up of *NDO* players – was the resident group, and Stuart was interviewing Derek, he asked him how he started in the business; I got a great thrill when he said that I had been an inspiration and influence throughout his musical career. I still book him to do gigs for me these days, but if I want to wind him up, I remind him that he still can't play jazz as good as I used to!

It was through Derek that I met James Shepherd, one of the world's best cornet players. He was principal cornet with the *Black Dyke Mills* band at the time and was feeling a little restricted musically. He, just like Derek before him, wanted to broaden his playing, which eventually led to him forming what became the famous brass group *Versatile Brass*, made up of top players from all the best brass bands in the country.

Before this came about though he asked me to do an arrangement of Lennon and McCartney's *Yesterday* for brass band, and he tried to get *Black Dyke* to use it but they didn't want to know, which is why I think Jim got frustrated with their attitude because it wasn't long before *Versatile Brass* came into existence. He suggested that as I had spent time doing the arrangement, I should take it to the *Yorkshire Imperial Metals Band*, another fine band but probably more broad-minded, or should I say a little less conservative than *Black Dyke*.

I took it to them and they liked it so much they even put it on one of their LPs. I developed a good relationship with the *IMP*'s band and their MD Trevor Warmsley. A bit later my big band did several joint concerts with them in Huddersfield Town Hall and Sheffield City Hall. It featured both bands playing their own repertoires and then coming together as one unit. I did about six arrangements of various pieces, including a concert arrangement of *McArthur Park* and *Here's That Rainy Day*, which was a transcription of the version done on the recording *Urbie Green and Twenty One Trombones*. I also did the Beatles' *Hey Jude*. My friend Bill Charleson did a medley of Michel LeGrand tunes. These concerts were a great success and I think it was the first time a brass band and a swing band had played together as one unit. I know it has been done since, but I was the first.

The guy I just mentioned, Bill Charleson, is a very fine musician who still plays for me whenever I need a saxophone player, be it alto or tenor, it doesn't matter which, he can do it. He is now retired, having been employed at the Leeds College of Music passing on all his experience of the music business to the good young players of the future. We have been friends a long time, playing in various bands together. He still does arrangements for people, and still plays jazz very well. He is also the musical director of a big band called *Manhattan Sound*.

Ronnie Bottomley, the first name mentioned in this tome, is a drummer I use a lot and again is another musician who teaches at the college turning out some good young drummers. He is a very happy sort of guy and is always good for a laugh. He was resident at Wakefield Theatre Club at the same time as I was at Batley. He is also very proud of the fact that he is a very good friend of one of the world's greatest drummers, Jeff Hamilton.

Another drummer who played for me in the early days is Francis Haywood. He is someone who before coming to me, the biggest band he had played with was an organ! I gave him his first chance to play with a band and he took it. Franny is a player who drives a band hard and takes no prisoners! Since those days he has been the drummer for many star names including Peter Gordino and Jim Davidson and was with Jim when they were the first entertainers to go and entertain the troops in the Falklands.

Other good instrumentalists who played for me at this time included Derek Harper, Maurice Schofield, Dickie Hawdon, Ronnie Baron, Brian Tann, Ken Hubbard, Fred Kelly, Colin Yates, Keith Baldwin, Basil Theabolds and Eric Smith in the trumpets. Alan Hemsworth, Grenvill Richmond, Geoff Soar, Gordon Beaumont, Vernon Ledgard, Tony Smith, Roy Allot, Harry Burgess and Stuart Wilson in the trombone section. In the sax section I used Alan Parkinson, Harold Robinson, Mike Cox, Joe Markey, Stan Aylott, Mike Schofield, Dave Wheatley, Ronnie Varo and Vernon Heap. Peter Kitson, Malcolm Blamires, Fred Barmingham and Brian Ibbotson all played piano for me at one time or another, Peter Finch, Jeff Loriman and Glen Allot played bass and before Franny Haywood, Ken Newton, Derek Walton and Dave Tyas had played drums. I didn't always use guitar but when I did it was either Mike Riley or Trevor Holdroyd and later Teddy Platt.

On our arrival back at Batley after recording *Opportunity Knocks* on the Sunday afternoon, Lulu opened at the club that evening and as our coach drew into the car park at about midnight, people were leaving and complaining about the show, saying how bad it had been, a few of them were asking for a refund. We later learned that she had just arrived back in the country after a long flight and was jet lagged. To be fair, she was fine the rest of the week.

HAROLD FIELDING'S

SUNDAY NIGHT

at the

BLACKPOOL OPERA HOUSE

Licensee and General Manager: D. Gledhill   House Manager: Leslie Heyes

Sunday, 29th June, 1975, at 6.10 and 8.20 p.m.

STUART ATKINS and THE OPERA HOUSE CONCERT ORCHESTRA

THE SONG SPINNERS

JOE 'Mr. PIANO' HENDERSON

THE NOLAN SISTERS

INTERVAL

CHARLIE WILLIAMS

JOE 'MR. PIANO' HENDERSON

One of the busiest piano men in Europe must surely be Scotsborn Joe Henderson. As a composer, Joe's piano solos have been recorded by his friendly 'rivals' in Britain—Bobby Crush; Mrs. Mills; Tony Hatch; Winifred Atwell and Russ Conway. His songs have been recorded by stars from all over the world, including Cliff Richard; Anthony Newley; Engelbert Humperdinck; Petula Clark; Jerry Lewis; George Hamilton IVth, and dozens of others. Joe himself is a prolific recording artiste. At the moment he has no less than 26 albums to his credit, and is now hard at work on his 27th! His umpteenth single is another of Joe's own compositions, called "The Eli Brackett Rag". The "Joe Henderson Show" has been a firm favourite on Radio Two for the past five years, and 'Mr. Piano' keeps cropping up as guest star on many TV programmes, year after year. Joe, born in Glasgow and reared in Kirkcaldy in Fifeshire, now divides his life as equally as possible between his 'get-away-from-it-all' thatched country cottage on the borders of Leicestershire/ Warwickshire and Northamptonshire and his office overlooking London's Kensington Gardens.

SUNDAY NIGHT AT THE OPERA HOUSE

at 6.10 and 8.20

HAROLD FIELDING *presents*

July 6th

The Bachelors · Rod Hull & Emu

WALTER LANDAUER · WILD HONEY

July 13th

Ken Dodd · Kenny Ball & His Jazzmen

JOHNNY HART · THE SONG SPINNERS

July 20th

Lena Zavaroni · Frank Carson

JOE HENDERSON · JOHNNY LISTER

July 27th

The Grumbleweeds · Tammy Jones

NORMAN COLLIER · THE REFLECTIONS

TICKETS £1.25 : £1 : 40p.   OPERA HOUSE BOX OFFICES

Printed by CITY PRINT (Milton Keynes) LTD., Simpson Rd., Bletchley, Milton Keynes MK1 1BA

Chapter Eight

Kings Of Comedy

Tommy Cooper.

I know that having read that name, you now have a smile on your face. Why? Because he was probably one of the funniest people who ever lived. A giant of a man with big feet, usually at an angle of ten to two, with a nervous laugh at the same time as messing up magic tricks. Yes, the tricks were messed up but in reality that was all part of the act; he was in fact a first class magician.

Tommy was booked to appear at the end of what was to be six weeks of comedy. Starting with two weeks of Morecambe and Wise, followed by two weeks of Norman Wisdom and finishing with two weeks of Tommy Cooper. Although we didn't know it at the time, fate was to take a hand in the first week of the run because this was the time that Eric Morecambe had his first heart attack. It happened on the Thursday evening of the first week as he was driving back to Leeds after the show.

On the Sunday of their opening, Ernie turned up for band call at the usual time of two-o'clock with his wife and a young man and woman who were dancers, and did various 'walk-ons' throughout the act. Eric didn't arrive until the evening show, which was quite normal for double acts, one of them usually looked after the musical side of things, after all the band call was for just what it implies, it isn't a rehearsal, it is to familiarise the band with the music and the running of the act.

The first time I saw Eric was in the interval of that evening's show. I had just left the band room and was walking along the corridor back-stage. He was hanging around having a cigarette and he looked at me, smiled and said; "'ow d'yer do" and I just burst out laughing; let's face it, there is nothing funny about that greeting, but it was he who was funny, just him, without even trying.

They went on stage that evening and they were marvellous, a lot of the stuff we were familiar with but it still made us all laugh. The two dancers were brilliant, never letting their faces slip while everyone was falling about with laughter. Eric called them something like Gladys and Fred; they did a fabulous Spanish gipsy dance and all the while Eric was taking the mickey, but never once did they corpse. This was the only time I was ever not able to play for laughing.

The place was packed out every evening with everyone rocking with laughter. Then on the Friday morning of that week I got a call from the club asking me, along with the rest of the band to go in for a meeting. We all arrived at about eleven o'clock and we were told that Eric had had a heart attack on his way back to the hotel the night before. We were all stunned and didn't quite take in what had happened. Ernie arrived with his wife and we all sat around discussing what should happen with the show. It was obvious Ernie wasn't going to be able to go on that night, as an act such as theirs had evolved over many years, and one without the other was not what the fans expected. He was devastated and had the look of someone who had no idea what to do.

As it turned out, Eric did recover, and they went on to work together for many more years, and in my humble opinion, made some of their best TV programmes ever; written by Eddie Braben and produced be Earnest Maxin, but at that moment Ernie must have thought that his world was at an end. It is well documented what happened when Eric stopped the car and asked a guy to drive him to hospital, how when he was laid on the stretcher he was asked for his autograph. Only a person with the comic outlook of Eric Morecambe would see humour in a serious situation like that. Ted Rogers and Joan Turner stood in for Eric and Ernie for the rest of that week and the following week their places were taken by Joan Reagan.

Norman Wisdom opened as scheduled, and did the usual show that one would expect from him. Business-wise it was a good two weeks but I don't think there was anything particularly memorable about it. I have met Sir Norman many times since those days and accompanied him on the shows that take place at the Gala Dinners, which are a part of the Celebrity Golf Tour.

So, after four weeks Tommy Cooper finally arrived. I don't know why, but he never did a Sunday at Batley. Someone would do a 'one nighter' with the rest of the 'bill' for the week, and then Tom came and took over from the Monday.

He turned up for band call at about five o'clock and we were all there to rehearse, sitting there on stage, instruments at the ready. Tom walked on and invited us all into his dressing room, saying; "Before we start lads, let's have a drink". So we all had a whisky and there was the usual chit-chat, and after about twenty minutes I said; "Shall we start the band call Tom?" He replied; "tell you what, we'll just have another, shall we?" So we had another drink.

This went on for quite a while until I realised that it was now almost half past seven, and we hadn't struck a note of music. Not only that, the patrons would start arriving at a quarter to eight, so I said; "Tom, we need to rehearse now, or the doors will be opening soon, and we won't be able to do it," so he said; "tell you what lads, just play me on with *The Sheik of Araby*, tha'r'll be aw' right!" It wasn't the longest band call I ever did, but it was one of the happiest!

Tommy always had with him a lady who looked after and prepared his props. She would set them all out on a table in their designated positions ready for the show. Before the curtain went the band would be in position ready to play and Tom would come to the table and for about five minutes he would fiddle about with these props, moving them around and making that little laugh with which we were all familiar. If you thought he was funny on stage, he was even funnier back-stage. By the time the curtain went up, for all of Tom's re-arranging, the props were in exactly the same places they had been from the start!

One of the props was a gate that was made for him by Alan Clegg, the club manager, and every now and then, Tom would just walk through it for no particular reason, and thereafter he used that gate in his act wherever he played. The compère would announce; "Ladies and Gentlemen – Tommy Cooper" and Tom would then ruffle the curtain before it opened, giving the impression that he couldn't get through, saying "wo's gone wrong now?" "wo's gone wrong now?" and the audience would start laughing even before the curtains opened. You wouldn't believe how many people have said to me, when recalling the days at Batley, "I was there that night when Tommy Cooper couldn't get on stage, do you remember"? Of course, I say "oh yes, I do". Great days!

A few years later when I was working with my wife Patti at Blazers Club in Windsor, Tommy was top of the bill, and every night just after she had gone on stage, Tom came and sat in the wings, watched the act and went back to his dressing room just before the end. At the end of the week his assistant came to her and said, "Mr Cooper sends his best wishes and to tell you that he enjoyed your act very much." Very nice of him wasn't it!

Two other comics I enjoyed working with were Harry Seacombe and Michael Bentine. I had always been a fan of the goons and to eventually work with two of them was a great thrill. Harry had a terrific voice as well as being very funny and Michael had a penchant for the absurd; he was also a very deep thinker and claimed that he knew at the exact minute when his son died in an air accident.

Chapter Nine

I Think He's Waving At Us!

I have played under many musical directors, some good and some not so good. I think the best was probably Roy Rogasin, Johnny Mathis' MD. I learned a lot about conducting by watching them whilst sitting in an orchestra. I think I learned as much from the poor ones as I did from the good ones. You see, when you're playing with a group of people, you need to be able to interpret what the MD wants from you. After all, the orchestra is the conductor's 'instrument', and how it performs is all down to the person in front waving their arms about. They must be clear in their movements, keeping the players informed as to which beat in the bar they are at, also keeping control of the dynamics, whether it needs to be loud or soft, or to slow it down or move it on, these things are all dependent on the conductor.

One time when Clodagh Rogers came to the club; she was pretty big at the time with several hits and a Eurovision Song Contest under her belt. She brought with her a young man who was a good pianist, but hadn't a clue when it came to directing. Well, Dickie Hawdon, the lead trumpet player, and I gave this lad quite a hard time because no one could follow what was required. When you have a twelve-piece band playing for a singer, someone has to take charge. I'm afraid the lad wasn't up to it. After a long rehearsal we managed to get somewhere near.

Our contention was that someone of Clodagh Rogers' standing in the business, at that time, should have brought with her a competent musical director. It wasn't really the lad's fault, because good pianist though he was, he had never directed before, but one of the top venues in the country wasn't the place to learn. Miss Rogers was out of order.

I came in contact with this pianist a few years later, his name was Pete Kelly (where have I heard that before?) and he told me that, at the time Dickie and I had done him the best favour anyone ever had, and he thanked me for it. Since then he had conducted West End shows. Another success for Hawdon and Atkins!

After all the palaver with the band call, we opened on the Sunday evening, which was in the height of summer and it was very hot. After the second number Clodagh turned to the band and said; "Do you want to take off your jackets, gentlemen?" And while all the other players took off their jackets, Dickie and I looked nonplussed with a shrug of the shoulders, more or less indicating that whatever the majority thought we'd go along with. We'd been round the block a few times you see, and comfort used to be secondary to appearance. We had to grin and bear it! However, it turned out that all the other players had been told that this was going to happen, but for some reason, the message hadn't been passed on to the two 'bolshie buggers' on the back row who had given the MD such a hard time in the afternoon. When 'Madame' came off stage she threw a tantrum, accusing us of behaving badly and being unprofessional. I would have thought that keeping jackets ON was by far more professional than removing them on stage! In fact, it was really nothing but a misunderstanding.

A few years later I was taking rehearsals at the ABC Theatre in Blackpool, for Cool Breeze and Clodagh was in the show with the girls; it was the Mike and Bernie Winters' summer season show, and we had a 'clear the air' chat and had a laugh about it. We called a truce and became good friends after that.

Brian Fahay was another very good MD who had been part of the London music scene for many years and was very well respected. He would start his rehearsal with the words; "OK folks, we don't need anyone to make a name for themselves" meaning, just play what's required and don't try to show off. After his stint with Shirley Bassey he became musical director of what was then the new *Scottish Radio Orchestra.* He is also a well-known composer; one of his more famous pieces is *At the Sign of the Swinging Cymbal.* If the title doesn't mean much to you, it will when I tell you it was the signature tune of Alan Freeman's *Pick of the Pops.* Yes?

Geoff Love was another famous conductor I was fortunate to play for. I forget who he came to the Batley Variety Club with, but one thing I do remember is that he offered me a job, saying "when are you coming to London". I told him I wasn't planning on going to London and he said; "that's a pity, because I could use you on some of my sessions", which was very nice of him. I think I must have impressed because I had to play a sixteen bar jazz solo in one of the arrangements. I was very flattered because I knew that before he became a conductor, he had made his name as a trombonist with Harry Gold and his *Pieces of Eight*. A series of Harry Gold's Dixieland arrangements were published and all the written solos were prefixed by; "*as played by*" – and then the name of the soloist, be it the trumpet player or whoever, and the trombone part always said; "*as played by Geoff Love*". I never took him up on his offer, as I was happy where I was. He was another Yorkshirman, born in Todmorden.

Frank Ifield brought Stan Reynolds to conduct for him. Stan was a trumpet player who had been in the great *Ted Heath Orchestra*, in its hey day.

Brian Fitzgerald was the pianist with the *NDO* and he came to MD for Des O'Connor. When Brian became the regular conductor of the *NDO*, the piano chair was taken by my very good friend Tom Steer. Tom came to Batley to MD for Carl Wayne and in my opinion, is the best pianist I have ever played with or have had play for me. He was one of the pianists in the orchestra when I conducted *Barnum* at Manchester Opera House in 1984, and along with Dave Lynaine on bass, Teddy Platt on guitar, and Ronnie Bottomley on drums, made up the best rhythm section my big band has ever had!

Johnny Hawkins, mentioned earlier along with Stuart Damon and Cool Breeze, is a good MD, a good pianist and a good saxophone player. I believe as a teenager he was a winner of the All Britain Accordion Championships. A right clever Dick wasn't he! He was Cilla Black's MD for a long time. John is a very good arranger; not all musical directors are arrangers, but he is, and a very good one too, especially for strings. Gracie Fields' pianist was Bert Waller, a very well known BBC session player.

Sid Boatman was the MD for Dickie Valentine. Dickie was a

very pleasant man without any edge whatsoever; in fact I was struck by his humility. We augmented the band for him with another trumpet and two more sax players, one of them, Vernon Heap, arrived on stage with his instrument under his arm and Dickie immediately went over to him and said; "Hello, I'm Dickie Valentine; I'm pleased to meet you". Ok, so it's a natural thing to do, but not many big stars would behave like that, I'm sure most would take for granted that anybody would know who they were.

Unfortunately, Dickie and Sid were killed in a car accident when returning home after a gig at the Double Diamond Club in Caerphilly. It was a very sad loss. Rod Palmer, a friend of mine, was his drummer at the time, but I believe he was on two weeks holiday when this happened. Had this not been so, it is more than likely he would have been involved also. How fortunate for him!

Dickie was not only a great singer in his own right, having learned his trade in the great *Ted Heath Band*, alongside Lita Roza and Denis Lotis, but was an excellent impressionist, being able to sound like many of the big names such as Nat 'King' Cole, Tony Bennett, Frank Sinatra and the like. He is very much missed in show business. Dickie and Don Phillips together wrote *That Old Piano Rag* which was a hit in the late 50s.

Don Phillips came to Batley to accompany and direct for Kathy Kirby. Don was quite a nervous man and I'll never forget the look on his face when he saw Red Price arrive on stage with an arm full of instruments; he had a tenor saxophone, a flute, an accordion, a clarinet, a trombone and a euphonium. There were times during band spots when Red would play any one of these, but when Don saw him walking on with this lot, he just stood there open mouthed, and we all cracked up laughing.

Every night at the end of Kathy's show, an admirer, Geoffrey Gee, a Leeds business man, sent her a bouquet of red roses. I later got to know Geoffrey when I conducted all the Harold Fielding Sunday Concerts at the Blackpool Opera House. He, and his then wife Brenda, used to sit in the two centre seats of the front row immediately behind me in the orchestra pit at every show.

Bob Dixon, pianist and MD for Max Bygraves was a small chap who sat at the piano and laughed at all of Max's jokes every night. I think he must have been on some sort of a bonus for that, 'cos they began to wear a bit thin after a week! But having been with Max for years, I suppose he was on automatic pilot.

Max Bygraves was, and is, very good and certainly a star, but I have to say he is not my favourite person. The first time I played for him we doubled the Greasborough Club with BVC. The second time he arrived at band call direct from flying into Manchester from Australia, and asked James Corrigan if there was anywhere he could get his suit valeted for the show. I'm afraid Batley doesn't have a big call for valet services on a Sunday afternoon! However, James knew that I had been a tailor, (in a previous life!) and told Max, who asked me if I could press his suit for the evening's performance; no problem! I took the suit home with me between band call and show time. I gave it a good press. It was fine. I arrived back at the club at seven o'clock and hung the suit in Mr.B's dressing room and left it. At eleven o'clock, I was taking up my place on the bandstand and Max Bygraves was standing next to me in the wings; he never said a word, no thank you, no nothing, not even "kiss my a—" we won't even go there! I have never thought much of him since that day.

Chapter Ten

A Galaxy Of Stars

In its time, I suppose Batley played host to more big names of the entertainment world than any other venue; it was the first of the big theatre clubs, but it wasn't the swankiest, I guess when someone starts a trend others follow and, with the benefit of hindsight, improve upon the original, but Batley always had the best 'feel' about it to perform in. When I was MD for the Bachelors in 1978 we were booked there for Easter week and even though it was starting to look a little bit faded, it still had the atmosphere about it that none of the other theatre clubs had. It closed within a few months of our booking there; meaning that in effect the Bachelors opened it and more or less closed it!

In between, it had all kinds of performers on its stage including Cliff Richard, who brought the Shadows with him; they had Alan Hawkshaw (he wrote the *Countdown* signature tune) on keyboards, a Leeds lad who played in the original *Bill Marsden Orchestra*, also Bruce Welch, John Farrar and Brian Bennett on drums. Cliff's road manager was David Brice, a very nice man, but that's no surprise as his brother was Dickie Valentine!

Olivia Newton John did the opening night with Cliff; she was with the same management and I think they wanted to try her out with a live audience. One thing I remember about her; she struggled to get into a song after a four bar introduction! She'd improved a little when I saw her in *Grease*!

Freda Paine had a big hit with *Band of Gold*; she was a super singer, leaning more towards jazz than pop with excellent arrangements. Bobby Rydell was a singer who had hits with *Volare* and the old Billy Daniels hit *That Old Black Magic*. His arrangements were good to play and he turned out to be a lovely friendly guy. He was a real swinger in the Sinatra style.

Another singer I liked was Guy Mitchell. He turned up without some of his band parts; luckily he had the piano parts with him so we were able to cobble something together before the show. After the Sunday performance there was a possibility of Dick Katz, the booking agent and Corrigan sacking him but we managed to persuade them to hold fire. So I took the piano parts home and I spent all Monday arranging the songs for the rest of the band. It worked and I got to play all those famous Mitch Miller horn parts on trombone!

One person I wasn't keen on was Buddy Greco, which was a pity because I have the greatest respect for him as a performer. I like his 'hip' style of singing, his piano playing and he is a good all round musician. I even have some of his CDs, but I found him to be very arrogant. He had a very 'big-time' attitude and he let us know that he was a big 'Hollywood Star'! Maybe the fact that he had been the pianist in the great *Benny Goodman Orchestra* made him feel that way. A while later I did a 'dep' at Wakefield Theatre Club with him, he remembered me and was very friendly but my first impression still persists! One enjoyable part of the Greco week at Batley was that Jimmy Blakemore was his drummer and what a terrific player he is. The last time I saw Jimmy he was touring with Jack Jones. Now he is someone I do like!

I never actually played for Mr Jones but I was introduced to him by Jerry Stevens who was touring with him at the time. I had dropped off an arrangement I had done for Jerry, which he was doing in the show and JJ seemed like a very nice person, engaging me in a long conversation and appearing to be genuinely interested.

Tony Orlando did a one nighter one Wednesday. I think his record company was testing the water with a new *Dawn* release. Lovelace Watkins was a big name on the club circuit for about three years and then seemed to disappear all at once. He was a very forceful performer, big in stature, an American black man with golden hair! His MD was Danny Sandage who had played alto saxophone with the *Stan Kenton Band*.

Neil Sedaka was a favourite with the Batley Variety Club audiences, in fact, his career was in the doldrums at the time and it was through playing Batley on quite a few occasions that seemed to be the start of the upturn in his fortunes.

The first time Tony Christie appeared at the club he was just another support act. He turned up for band call and prior to rehearsal, he was with us all in the band room watching the 1970 World Cup from Mexico. Even in those days I was sure that he would go on to have a successful career. Later we would both have the same management.

One of the most quirky acts we had was Tiny Tim, a six-foot-three American with matted dirty hair, bad breath, a scruffy appearance and a voice that sounded like a wolf howl. He had a hit with *Tip Toe Through the Tulips*, remember? One evening a drunk managed to get on stage and took a poke at him, I don't know if the guy was upset by his voice or his looks. In reality, he was probably a music lover!

One person I could never forget is Dorothy Squires, not so much for her singing but for her swearing ability. She would not have been out of place down a mine, in a barrack room or a band room for that matter. She could hold her own with anyone when it came to the expletive stakes. Her MD was a young man called Kenny Brown. One evening after the show the Deb Set took Kenny to their home for supper and unfortunately he had Ms Squires' car keys in his pocket. The phone rang and the biggest load of disgusting language you ever heard came down the line, turning the air red hot, it's a wonder poor Kenny's ear didn't catch fire!

We had some great singing groups including The Drifters, The Stylistics, The Searchers, Gerry and the Pacemakers and The Three Degrees, whose manager – a nasty piece of work – always carried a gun; the girls were terrified of him. Another group that always did well was The Hollies; what I admired about them was their confidence in their own pulling power because they weren't paid a fee, they took a percentage of the door. The public responded because they were very good. A few years later I was booked on trombone to do a national tour with them and I shall never forget their drummer Bobby Elliot. We were playing the Philharmonic Hall in Liverpool and Pat had gone with me. She was sitting in the stalls at the run through (for sound check) and Bobby saw her, even though he had only seen her when she was a dancer at BVC in the early days, he made a point of going to her and saying

"Hello Pat, how are you?" Nice!

One other group I should mention: The Bee Gees. They took from Batley more than their fee; they took away a wife for Maurice! Yvonne Spencley worked in the booking office and it was here that they met and fell in love. When I see Yvonne on TV since the death of Maurice I feel so very sorry for her, but I'm also happy for her because she appears to have a loving family around her.

One very entertaining group was The Carols; this group was made up of four brothers and their sister Irene from Liverpool. They sang and danced very well and Irene did very good impressions. She eventually left her brothers to carry on with the act and she went solo. She changed her name to Faith Brown!

We had the show groups; these were the ones who didn't just sing but did comedy and impressions. They included the Rocking Berries, Baron Knights, Black Abbots, the Cresters – who featured the drummer who was to become one of the funniest people on TV – Johnny Casson, and brothers John and Richard Harding. Richard is a great guitar player! The Dallas Boys were a very good act. As well as doing good comedy routines, their singing was very good; their five part harmonies were excellent. But the best of them all for me had to be the Grumbleweeds.

Of the double acts, there was Mike and Bernie Winters; very talented and very good professionals. Mike was a good clarinet player and Bernie played the drums. Daly and Wayne were very popular, as were Lester and Smart and two acts that were just starting to become known were Sid and Eddie, who had changed their name to Little and Large and two lads who had been called the Harper Brothers had now become Cannon and Ball.

Scarborough Opera House 1980 The Grumbleweeds Show

There were a lot of unsung acts who made up the various bills; good singers such as Eddie Buchanan, who did quite a few Benny Hill TV shows, Dean Raymond who had been featured singer with the *Vic Lewis Orchestra,* Pat O'Hare, who did thousands of broadcasts with the *NDO*, and there were some good girl singers too. Gail West, Wendy King, who also played banjo, Lori Wells, Lorne Leslie (now David Dickinson's wife), Lena Storm and a young lady called Tansy did a week. The next time we saw Tansy was when she came back as a member of the New Seekers, this time under her other name- Lyn Paul! Lyn was one of many support acts who went on to become well known in their own right.

A lot of good comics went on to make a name for themselves after working at Batley. Among them were Norman Collier, famous for his chicken routine, Tony Dowling, who left showbiz and set up a string of video shops; I believe he now lives in Florida. Bernie

Clifton played there, long before he found the ostrich. Jim Bowen; this was before he even knew what a dartboard looked like! Dougie Brown, not only a comedian, also a character actor, and he just happened to be the brother of Lynn Perry, who appeared with us and went on to play Ivy Tylsley in *Coronation Street*. Bobby Pattinson was a very fine Geordie comic, Pat Moony, the Irishman with the green suit, Mick Miller, the Max Wall look-a-like, Max Wall himself, Mike Lancaster, Ken Goodwin, George Roper, Charlie Williams; this was his first real big break, and Jerry Stevens, whom Ernest Maxin put together with Lennie Bennett to form a double act to introduce the TV series from the Talk of the Town. Lennie himself also did many shows at the club.

There were also some super 'spesh' acts including Paul Daniels whose name in those days appeared on the bill below the printer! Great ventriloquists; Arthur Worsley, the very funny Neville King, Tony Adams and in my opinion the greatest vent who ever lived: Ray Allen.

A lot of these people, who were supports in those days at BVC, went on to become household names, and I still see many of them. I'm happy to say we remain good friends, from all those years ago.

The one performer who played Batley more than any other was an Australian hypnotist called Martin St James. He was very popular and had a big following. He always filled the place and never failed to entertain. I think he did over one hundred and fifty shows at Batley. Because of his popularity YTV made a series of programmes with him at their studios in Leeds. They used our band, at Martin's request, because the act was such that nothing was set and the music had to match what was being done by the people who were reacting to Martin's orders, whilst being under hypnosis. Because we had played the act so many times, we knew which tunes to play for whatever was taking place on stage.

Batley Variety Club was good to me, it opened a lot of doors for me and I met and made friends with a lot of people. I was employed there full time from 1968 to 1973. But I worked there on and off right up to its closing in '78. I would do a week on trombone or a week on piano, and then I'd be away working on the road. Life was good, and never boring! The reason I left was because I was offered a job by Phillip Solomon.

Roy Orbison was top of the bill and it was his closing night. In the interval someone called me to take a phone call; it was Phil Solomon, and he said; "Do you remember when we signed the girls (Cool Breeze), we talked about you doing some things with the office?"

I said "Yes."

"Well," he said, "I want an MD/Arranger for all the acts on our books, would you like to work for us?"

I was a bit surprised and said, "Could I have a think about it?"

"Oh that's a pity," he replied. "I wanted you to go to Mexico on Friday."

I immediately said, "I'll do it!"

This was when I could play!

Chapter Eleven

In At The Deep End

It was Friday 22nd November 1972 and I'm sitting in an Aero Mexico 707 plane, thirty-five thousand feet above the Atlantic and it suddenly hit me; what the hell is going on? Seven days ago I received a phone call and it is about to make another direction change to my career. I started to think about what had happened to me in the past seven days. After the show on the Saturday, I told James Corrigan what had happened and asked him if I could put in a 'dep' for the next two weeks; no problem, I told him all about it and he was pleased for me. Come Monday morning I was on my way to London. The reason for the Mexican trip was for me to conduct for Neal Reed who was to perform at the Augustine Lara Song Festival in Mexico City.

Augustine Lara was a Mexican poet and, although he was dead, the festival was named in his honour. He wrote the lyrics to the Perry Como hit *It's Impossible*. Neil Reid on the other hand, was a twelve-year-old Scottish kid who had won *Opportunity Knocks* a record number of weeks, and was signed to the Dorothy Solomon Agency. They had provided him with a recording contract and he had been lucky enough to have a world-wide hit with a song called *Mother of Mine*. Because of this he had been invited to perform on the International Gala along with a guest list that included Tony Hatch and Jackie Trent, Les Reed, Roger Cook (the one from Blue Mink, not the investigative TV reporter!), and Cal Tchada, a famous American jazz vibraphone and harmonica player.

During that week I had to get a passport from the Petite France Passport Office; as this was the first time I had been abroad, apart from Jersey, but that doesn't count, does it! I stayed in Edgware with Bryan Savoury, who was a road manager for the Solomon office. So now I was just beginning to realise what was happening. It was very exciting really.

We landed at the airport, which is in the shadow of Popacatapetal, the famous volcano, and we were transported to the Camino Real Hotel. I'd never seen anything like it, talk about opulence, it was fabulous. It was only three storeys high but it was built in the style of an Aztec Pyramid. After checking in I thought I'd do a 'recce', and as I looked around there was a point where I bounded up a flight of stairs; bad move! When I got to the top of the steps I thought I was having a heart attack, I was breathless and had to sit down for a while. You see I'd completely forgotten that we were at about five thousand feet altitude, and oh boy, didn't that remind me! It was quite surprising though how quickly we got used to it.

In the two weeks we were there we only had to do one concert, most of the time was taken up with promotional work. However, as I had never seen what Neil's act consisted of I thought I had better familiarise myself with it.

We got together around a piano and went through the seven numbers he was to perform and knowing what musicians are like – remember the Clodagh Rogers MD story? – I told him that he must go with me whatever happens. I didn't realise at this point, it was going to be an eighty-piece symphony orchestra! So, I went in strong, this was the deep end, waving the baton in a flamboyant and confident way and it worked, I gained their respect. Thank goodness! Had I shown any weakness or naivety they would have had me for breakfast. The show itself was a great success and I was very impressed with Neil Reid who, for a twelve-year-old performed with a lot of maturity.

I enjoyed my stay in Mexico City. Dorothy Solomon came out for the show and Margaret Adams, who worked in the office, acted as Neil's chaperone. When Dorothy went back to London, in between the promo thing, we did the tourist bit. Taking in the *Mexican Folk Ballet*, which was fantastic and visiting the Aztec Pyramids, fabulous! Oh yes, and at thirty-five years old I learned to swim! On the middle Sunday evening we went to a place where there are about forty cantinas around a piazza, and several mariachi bands playing. This is a local Sunday evening ritual, where gentlemen take their sweethearts and they pay the bands to play a romantic song for their lovers; all very romantic!

On arriving home from Mexico I went back to the Variety Club and stayed there 'till January '73. I then told James that I was leaving to take up Phil Solomon's offer. I moved to London five days a week, coming home to Yorkshire at the weekend. I now moved in on a more permanent basis with Bryan Savoury.

In early February we went to the *Yamaha Song Festival* in Tokyo. We flew over the North Pole on a JAL Jumbo jet, passing over the highest mountain in North America, Mount McKinley, with a stopover at Anchorage. This time Neil's father who had given up his job as a woodwork teacher came along as chaperone and, unfortunately, was something of an embarrassment. He had come along to replace Margaret Adams. The thing was, Margaret could talk to agents and producers on the same level, but this man had no idea about show business at all. I think he was rather jealous of all the attention his son was getting and wanted a bit of it. I know that once when Neil was in *Harrods*, he was asked for his autograph by a crowd of young girls and his dad also signed - as 'Neil Reid's father'. What a pillock! Enough of that, back to the music. Again, I was conducting an eighty-piece orchestra; in the Budokan Hall, it was great! What an aphrodisiac it is to stand in front of a large orchestra and have them react to your every movement. It is a fantastic ego trip! We were in Tokyo for three weeks and, as well as the festival, we did promotional work. We stayed at the Pacific Hotel, which is directly opposite the main station. My room was on the nineteenth floor and I used to watch the packers pushing people on to the urban trains. This was the station that the Bullet Train left from on which we went to Osaka and Kobe; it was just like being in an aircraft. About an hour out of Tokyo we looked to our right and there was Mount Fuji. They say whenever you see a picture of anything Japanese, Mount Fuji is always there, and it was!

The promotions took the form of doing shows in the music sections of the huge department stores of the Ginza district. This is the main shopping area of Tokyo. These shows would take place at midday; and with a twelve-piece band! We would perform to shoppers and office workers taking their lunch breaks. We did the same thing in Osaka and Kobe.

We flew back to Tokyo on a 747 which was virtually empty. Air travel wasn't as popular then as it is now and planes were very rarely full in those days. On our return to Tokyo I went with Tony Christie, who was also on the festival, to record some songs just for the Japanese market. One of which was *Is This the Way to Amarillo*. I believe his record company was a bit miffed at him for doing this song, because all his hits had been written by Peter Callander and Mitch Murray up to then, and this was written by Neil Sedaka.

Whilst in Tokyo, one thing I did come across for the first time was karaoke; it was in all the restaurants and usually it was middle-aged Japanese businessmen who were taking part. It was quite funny because we were hearing songs like *Fry Me to da Moon* and *Flom Lussia wiv Ruv*!

We arrived back in London in late February at the same time as the Bachelors arrived back from a five-week tour of Australia. They were very big at that time and went there about every two years. My first gig with them was in an Irish ballroom in Kilburn and their drummer was a guy called Arthur Dakin who was from Blackpool.

I now started to do all the Bachelors' work and, because they were a big name group, they could insist on a minimum size band of at least twelve pieces on their contracts at any venue they appeared at. I was enjoying myself, conducting all the time.

Come March, Dorothy had arranged for the Bachelors and Cool Breeze to perform at the *Bratislava Song Festival* in Czechoslovakia. Again it was a full orchestra, made up of the Czech National TV musicians augmented by the string section of the *Prague Symphony Orchestra.* This time, not only did I get to conduct such an aggregation, I had to do all the musical arrangements for it, my goodness, and all that lot to write for!

I had three weeks to prepare all the charts and I did it. I told you how exciting it is to conduct an orchestra that big. Well the biggest ego trip of all is when you hear the sound on the downbeat, and you yourself have written those notes coming from all those musicians. It's better than sex! Well, maybe not, but almost. To top it all at the end of the rehearsal the whole orchestra stood up and applauded me, I was almost in tears. In front of me was a nine piece rhythm section in the pit, with the brass, saxes and woodwind banked up on the right of me and the string section banked up on the left - wonderful! When you get a high like that, they take some following, but I did have a few more in my career!

All this took place after Dubcek had tried to take control from the communists. The Iron Curtain was still in place at this time. I recall one evening when Cool Breeze, Arthur Dakin and I had been for an evening stroll on the banks of the Danube. We came back to the hotel, which was in the main square and in the middle was a fountain. As we approached the fountain, Patsie said to Arthur "I bet you daren't jump in". How wrong could she be? Within seconds he'd stripped to his underpants and socks and was in the fountain. Just at that moment, two armed guards appeared and our laughter started to take on a hollow sound. The two guards motioned for Arthur to get out of the fountain, and took him up to the hotel room he was sharing with Bryan Savoury.

As the three of them went in the room, the two guards collapsed with laughter. The fortunate thing was that these two were Czech guards and saw the funny side of the situation, but had they been

Russian, Arthur would probably have become a drummer with the Symphony Orchestra of Siberia! Bryan gave the guards a bottle of whisky each and two hundred cigarettes. They went on their way very happy! This story was reported in the following Sunday's *News of the World* and *Sunday Times*.

I liked Arthur very much, he was a very happy and generous person; sadly he is no longer with us. He became a successful 'fixer' (*fixer* - someone who books musicians for shows, concerts, recording sessions etc.) and a few years ago he was taking the wages to one of his pantomime bands, somewhere in the West Country, when he was caught up in a flood and he drowned. He is very much missed in the business. One example of his generosity; when we arrived back at Heathrow from Bratislava and customs searched his drum cases; they found no sticks, no drum skins and no Latin 'toys'. He had given them all away!

Chapter Twelve

On The Nose

In four months I had done more travelling than my parents did in a lifetime. This brought home to me how lucky I was to be in the right place at the right time. It started the day at Batley Variety Club when the girls were rehearsing that song of mine, leading to the record contract, which led to the Solomon office, then to the phone call from Phil Solomon. In that time I'd been to Mexico, Japan and Czechoslovakia. It was hard to believe really. I would never have thought, as I blew my trombone during that Roy Orbison show, that in a few months I would have been half way round the world to places most people could only read about in newspapers, and conducted three symphony orchestras. I pinched myself, yes it was true!

Now we were back home and I was working with The Bachelors on their dates doing various clubs and theatres. They were due to do the summer season in Paignton and Phil Solomon offered me the MD's job but I didn't take it because I didn't think the money was good enough for me to live in Paignton and keep a home going in Wakefield. I continued to work with the boys until the season started then I came back home to Yorkshire. I did freelance work, still did the odd gig at Batley, still writing and conducting for Cool Breeze, and doing more work with the big band.

Bernard Hinchcliffe was now booking for us and quite a bit of work was starting to come our way. He booked us concerts, dances, Police Balls, Mayors' Balls, Hunt Balls and the like; that's a lot of balls, isn't it? He booked us four concert dates at the Auditorium in Palma, Majorca. We did a few cruises, the first being in the Mediterranean. We picked up the ship, *MV Ithaca*, in Brindisi on the south-east coast of Italy, taking in places such as Rhodes, Crete and Dubrovnik, but the place that stands out was Beirut where I saw the most spectacular live show I had ever seen. It was at the *Casino Du Liban* and produced by Charlie Henches from the *Paris Lido*. There were girls on steps which in a flash turned into waterfalls, Bedouin horsemen riding straight at the audience on fast treadmills, a moon buggy appearing from the ceiling, and elephants, tigers, giraffes and all manner of animals. It was quite breathtaking!

The last night of the cruise was memorable because we performed in a force eight sea swell and the show which started with the eighteen piece band, finished with a thirteen piece! We lost five players due to the conditions.

On another cruise, the Premier Drum Company had taken over the ship to reward all of their retailers, so our drummer, Francis Haywood, didn't have the bother of taking his kit because they provided one for him. We also did a tour backing The Bachelors, Cool Breeze, Lennie Bennett and Jerry Stevens. A little later we went on tour with Al Martino. Little did I think, when as a school kid listening to *Here in my Heart*, which was the first number one in the very first hit parade, that one day Stuart Atkins and his Orchestra would share a bill with Al Martino and provide the backing for him. We opened at the Theatre Royal, Drury Lane. This was at the time that Al was in the charts with *Spanish Eyes*.

Even though I didn't do the '73 season with The Bachelors I still did various gigs with them. One of which was for Combined Services Entertainments (CSE) in Gibraltar. This is the entertainment branch of the armed forces. During the Second World War it was known as ENSA. The guy in charge of CSE in those days was Major Derek Agutter who was a bit of a nutcase. I mean that in the nicest possible way. When he was around nobody slept, it was always party time! Yes, if you thought the surname was familiar, you are right, Jenny, the famous actress, is his daughter.

Also on the bill was Linda Myers, who sang and played trumpet, she was also very glamorous, singer Ray Merrill and the incomparable Norman Collier. Just like Tommy Cooper, Norman is one of these people that when you see them you automatically smile, he's a very funny man.

On arriving back from Gibraltar we went straight into The Talk of the Town in Leicester Square, where I was able to renew a few old acquaintances with some of the band including drummer Bobby Worth.

In 1974 The Bachelors did a summer season at the Floral Hall, Scarborough, but I didn't do it with them. I was still running the big band and was conducting the Sunday concerts at Blackpool Opera House for Harold Fielding Ltd. which I had been doing since 1972, and I continued to do so right up to them finishing in 1982.

Harold had been presenting twenty Sunday concerts a year at Blackpool every summer for thirty-two years. Starting on Easter Sunday and then Whit Sunday through to October, and had presented major artistes from the Vienna Boys Choir to Frank Sinatra in that time.

I got the job because when I had been to direct for Cool Breeze or The Bachelors whenever they had appeared on these concerts, I understand I made an impression on Jeanette Peters, who was the producer for Mr. Fielding. I learned later that she was struck by how quickly we got through the band calls. Danny Walters had been doing these concerts for a long number of years but he was now an old man and ready for retiring. When the time came, it appears Moira Anderson and Dorothy Solomon suggested to Jeanette that I maybe interested in doing the concerts, and she agreed, so when I was asked, I said yes!

The Fielding office was a very good firm to work for. In the first year they made me an offer which was very generous and every year after that they asked me to do the concerts for the coming season, and with a substantially raised offer, which was always acceptable.

When I was seventeen years old I went to Blackpool for a week's holiday with a group of pals. In those days, the early '50s, there were at least a dozen theatres presenting shows, and the premiere theatre was, and still is, the Opera House. I still have the programme from the Harold Fielding Sunday Concert I saw that week. On the front, with an orange boarder, is a photo of Guy Mitchell and inside is listed the cast which was; Douglas Maynard, The Stargazers, Bill McGuffie, Jill Day, and top of the bill, Guy Mitchell. It also says 'and the *Opera House Orchestra* conducted by Jack Ansell'. I never thought that at some point in the future my name would be where it said Jack Ansell, or that one day I would work with the main star.

A lot of very good performers did these concerts. We did the band call at two o'clock on the Sunday afternoon and two shows in the evening, six-ten, and eight-twenty. I remember one conversation I had with Walter Landauer, well known as half of the famous piano duettists Rawicz and Landauer. At this time Walter was a solo pianist, - as Rawicz had died a few years earlier - and he was congratulating me on my conducting; he told me that he used to give tips on piano playing to his friend, and in return, the friend taught Walter to conduct. Guess what; the friend was none other than Herbert von Karajan!

I remember doing a concert with The Bachelors in Llandudno and the band in the pit was made up of musicians who were basically semi-pro dance band players. At one point in the act, after a certain cue, the music starts to play and because it is immediate there is no time for a count in, so it starts on the down beat; this is known in the business as 'on the nose', and so that the musicians know where the down beat is, the conductor starts with an up-beat, then the band plays as the baton comes down. As the dialogue was going on, I was ready for a quick entrance of the music and kept giving the signal to the band to be ready by tapping my finger on my nose; this is a usual procedure and all professional musicians know what it means. As I was doing this, one of the trumpet players took out his handkerchief and started to wipe his nose, looking at me in a manner that suggested that he thought I was trying to tell him that he had something on his nose. The drummer, Tony Layzelle, and I could hardly contain ourselves and the boys on stage had noticed this; they also found it hard not to laugh!

I don't know where the term 'on the nose' comes from but I imagine it could be that when an MD is sitting at a piano, and to indicate to his musicians when to start; because he needs his hands to play he brings them in by raising his head and bringing it forward on the down beat; and because the nose is the focal point of the face, hence the phrase 'on the nose'. It sounds plausible anyway!

Musicians tend to have certain phrases which most other people wouldn't understand, for instance: if someone says to another "who's on stick"? It means who is the conductor, or if someone says "I'm depping for so and so" it means they are deputising for someone on a gig. Gig originally meant a booking for musicians, although today it has taken on a wider meaning; people will use it to say they are going to a club or a show.

Another gig we did was at a house party in Scotland at the home of a Norwegian industrialist and Prince Charles was the guest of honour. As well as the Bachelors, Marty Cain performed at this party and I had a band which included musicians from the *BBC Scottish Radio Orchestra*, including Brian Payne, who had been the bassist at Batley with me, Derek Brackpool, who took over the trombone chair from me at BVC, Frank Pantrini, a wonderful tenor sax player and Paul Eshleby, a very fine trumpet player from Thornton-le-Dale who used to augment the band for us at BVC while still a student at the Leeds Music College and went on to become a member of the *BBC Big Band*.

A few years later I remember reading in a newspaper article about a very messy divorce case which involved the ownership of a pair of very expensive gold and diamond cufflinks – about twenty five thousand pounds I seem to remember; the wife contended that she should have them because she bought them, but the husband said that he should have them because they were bought with his money anyway; the wife was awarded the cufflinks! I tell this story because these were the people who threw the party.

In March '76 I went on a cruise with Cool Breeze; we flew to Casablanca to pick up the ship, this time it was *MV Ulysses*, which wasn't quite as big as the *Ithaca*. We sailed down the West African coast calling at Dakar in Senegal. When we left the ship, as in most of these places, we were accosted by hordes of children holding out their hands for pennies, and although it can be heart breaking, if you give one, that's it, they're with you forever.

We did manage to get rid of them but one little lad was persistent, and he stayed with us and became our guide. He took us to various places of interest, including the local market where the girls bought beautiful multi coloured sarongs, in fact Patti still wears hers, so she can't complain about the quality! As we were walking back to the ship along this red dirt road the lad said, so very naturally, "I want a piss", and he did it just where he stood in the road. I think it is said: "Travel broadens the mind!"

After Senegal we called in The Gambia, where it was so hot we could hardly walk on the beach and Wendy's friend Laura got food poisoning after eating some local prawns. From there we went to Freetown in Sierra Leone, and then across to the Cape Verde Islands, which was a complete waste of time!

The cruise should have ended in Madeira but the weather was so bad that we were eleven hours behind schedule so the cruise terminated in Tenerife. On the way up to Tenerife, the girls did their final cabaret, which was rather hilarious. The ship was rolling from side to side and Rosemary and Wendy are taller than Pat and in high heels even more so. This meant that these two could reach up to the low ceiling of the room and wedge themselves. The funny part was that Pat was in the middle and as she sang, every time the ship rolled she would bounce off one or the other from side to side. One of the songs in the act was *With These Hands* and when it got to the line "should there be, a stormy sea, I'll turn the tide for you" it made it even funnier.

~*~

The Bachelors had asked me if I would like to conduct their summer season show at the Bournemouth Pavilion Theatre that year. This was to be presented by Robert Luff Ltd., who also owned the rights to the *Black and White Minstrels*. I said I would very much like to do it, so the deal was done; which was a lot better than the one offered by Phil Solomon for the Paignton season, and we opened just after Whitsuntide for twenty-two weeks. This length of season was quite the norm in those days, whereas today, if you do three consecutive days in one place, it's tantamount to a season!

The Bachelors who topped the bill were supported by Billy Dainty, a great observation comic, the Vernons, three girl singers, Corrine, Jackie, and Patsie - who is now Mrs Eddie Large, Johnny Stafford, a harmonica player, six chorus singers and twelve Tiller Girls. All this was backed by a twelve-piece band. What a show! Sadly, today it would be backing tracks or organ and drums!

Early in the year I had split with Shirley, and Pat and I had moved in with each other. We had only been together for two weeks when I went off to Bournemouth and she went to Scarborough, to do the season with Les Dawson. We saw each other at weekends when I arrived home at about three o'clock in the morning. Then come Sunday lunch time, I would go off to Blackpool Opera House and she would go and do a concert with Cool Breeze somewhere, then we would get home in the late evening, get up on Monday morning, have breakfast, clean teeth, set off back to our respective gigs, "'bye, see you next week, I'll ring later." What a carry on, and this went on all season!

That year was a very hot summer and as I conducted the orchestra in the pit, the audience could see my back and shoulders in my white jacket, but they didn't realize I was wearing shorts and standing in two bowls of cold water, one for each foot, because it was so hot. Some evenings after the show, a few of the girls went skinny-dipping in the sea, which was just across the road from the theatre. Many times that year basking sharks were seen close to the beach; it was so hot.

Socially the season was excellent. I had a good band made up of a lot of people I had worked with before. Ken Newton, who had played with me all those years at Batley was on drums, Glen Allot, who had done gigs with my big band, was on bass, Ted Platt, my good friend on guitar, and still plays with me after all this time. Peter Lingwood, just out of Leeds Music College played piano, and this was his first professional job; he later became percussionist and second keyboard to Tom Steer, with the *NDO*. In the trumpet section I had Big John Saunders, Bill Lymm, ex Joe Loss and Don Morgan, who was the son-in-law of one of my heroes, George Chisholm to whom I was later introduced by Don. My long time friend Gordon Beaumont was on trombone.

The Freddie Starr show was at the Winter Gardens Theatre, and both casts and bands used to meet after the shows at a club called *Bumbles*. Twice a week there would be a jazz session, and I used to take my trombone for a blow, just to keep my lip 'in'. A local trombone player called Dougie Smith used to go along to these sessions, and he and I used to play duets, which were enjoyed by us and very well received by everyone. Dougie also played bass and when our bass player became ill one time, he depped in the show.

Eddie Peacock was the MD of the show at the Winter Gardens, which included Lyn Paul, comedian Mike Burton and vent Jack O'Riley. I knew Eddie from the time he worked at many of the nightclubs in Yorkshire; he was very fond of cricket and used to organize matches between the two shows' companies. With the gorgeous weather and the lovely location, this was one of the most enjoyable seasons I ever did.

Patti and Freddie

Chapter Thirteen

The Bachelors:
The Thin End Of The Wedge

At the end of '76 Cool Breeze were booked to do the seven weeks Tommy Steele Twentieth Anniversary Tour. This took in all the towns he had played in the first week of his very first tour in show-biz. The show played a week in each of the places starting in Coventry, then on to Sunderland. I arranged all the music for the girls' new act, which was backed by a twenty-six piece orchestra. Cool Breeze, who opened the show, were followed by the Mosaics, an oversized UV (ultra violet light) puppet act, the Las Vegas magician Johnny Hart – a tiger was used in one of his tricks, and Lennie Bennett closed the first half. Tommy Steele did the whole of the second half.

I had worked with Tommy Steele before when I was part of the trombone section for his two weeks appearance at Wakefield Theatre Club in the early '70s. Then his MD was Clive Chaplin, now it was Allan Bence.

For various reasons Cool Breeze had had a few changes in personnel over the years. Rosemary, who started the group as the

Deb Set, and Pat being sisters were constant throughout the group's life. The third member of the act was now Wendy Balldock, whom the girls had first met in 1971 in a summer season with Frank Ifield in Great Yarmouth. Wendy was a good singer, an excellent dancer and was a great asset to the group.

When the show arrived at the Leeds Grand Theatre, one evening after the show we had a party at our home in Rothwell. Of course it didn't start 'till midnight and everyone from the show was there. Tommy arrived at our party, which seemed to go on forever, at about two o'clock and was the last to leave at about seven in the morning, after having had a bacon and egg sandwich and a strong coffee for breakfast.

The show was such a success that it went into the Festival Theatre, Paignton for a late summer season show in '77. This followed a mid season show featuring The Bachelors, which I conducted.

I was asked to do some work with the Irish lads again in early '77 and one of the weeks was at Glasgow Pavilion Theatre. While we were there the lads, who were good golfers took me to Grangemouth Golf Club, whose professional, John Black, was a friend of theirs. He sold me my first set of golf clubs, and then I got the bug. That was the thin end of the wedge! Once you have hit that first crisp shot out of the middle of a golf club, that's it, you become the biggest bore in the world; it's the last thing you think about before going to sleep and the first thing you think about on awakening!

In the summer we did two weeks at the Sandown Pavilion on the Isle of Wight. This came about because Ivor Emmanuel was the star of a six-month season, and he had an arrangement with the promoter that he would only do so long, if he could have a two week break in the middle. This was agreed and The Bachelors were booked to take Ivor's place for the two weeks.

When we arrived for the band call on the Monday morning a rather funny incident took place. The regular band for the season was a five piece, and if you remember, the Bachelors always had at least a ten piece. Well because the resident MD, Paul Mathews, had more musicians to work with, he had done new arrangements of all the music used in the show. Starting with a new overture, a new entr'acte (that's like the overture of the second half) and all the production numbers.

We had our own drummer with us; Tony Layzelle, who had taken Arthur Dakin's place, and it is normal practice that when an act with their own drummer goes on stage, the resident guy moves out and the other drummer slides on to the kit with the minimum of fuss. This was to take place after the entr'acte. It is usual in situations like this that the visiting player uses their own snare drum and sticks.

I have to point out that Paul Mathews had a very serious stammer, and it so happened that Tony had a slight stammer. It is a known fact that when people who do stammer get together, one will often set off the other person. Now, just as Tony was leaning over the pit wall arranging the changeover with the resident drummer, Paul stood up from the piano and said; "O.O.O.kkkk j...j...gentlemen we're g...g...going to pl...play *Sp...Sp...Sp...Spinn-ing Wheeeel*", at which point Tony was saying to the other drummer "I'll sl...sl...slide on af...aft...after th...th...the en...en...ent," and on hearing this Paul, not knowing that Tony had a slight problem also, said "h...h...here mate are y…y…you t…t…taking the p…p…p…" and Tony jumped in saying "n…n no, I, I, I……".

While all this was going on The Bachelors, Dave Wilkins, the roadie, and myself, sitting in the stalls, were falling about in fits of laughter. When they both realized the truth of the situation they themselves laughed about it. Paul and Tony became best drinking buddies for the next two weeks!

We finished our two weeks at the Pavilion and after the show on the Saturday night we caught the last ferry to Portsmouth. From there we made our way to the Roundhouse Hotel in Bournemouth where we stayed overnight before moving on to Torbay the next morning.

On arriving at the Princess Theatre in Torquay we had a quick run through of the show, which featured comedian Gordon Peters, singer Patsie McLean, Lord Charles, who as usual was assisted by Ray Alan, and a team of dancers. For some reason, which I don't remember, I finished up conducting the whole show, which was quite acceptable to me, and to The Bachelors, as it meant that my fee (which was increased) was split between them and John Redgrave the producer. We did a week at the Princess and then the whole show moved around the bay to do four more weeks at the Festival Theatre in Paignton.

I had conducted a few shows over the years at the Princess. I didn't know until it was pointed out to me, by the TV producer Earnest Maxin that the theatre is built the wrong way. How come? Well, the front of the theatre is facing west, and you walk from the foyer into the back of the auditorium. This means that on a summer's evening the sun shines through the doors, as people come in and go out, and through the control room windows, this contains the sound and lighting desks, and filters into the theatre.

I enjoyed these five weeks in Torbay, in the middle of which the Queen's Silver Jubilee Celebrations took place, and during this time my golf started to come on in leaps and bounds. I said earlier that I considered Ray Alan to be the world's best ventriloquist; this is because for the whole five weeks that I stood underneath him in the pit I never once saw his lips move, or for that matter his Adam's apple.

This was my first encounter with John Redgrave, who I believe is related to the famous acting dynasty. I was to come across him later in my career; and it wasn't always a pleasure!

The Bachelors were all good golfers, John Stokes had a handicap of four, Con Clusky's was six and his brother Dec's was eight; anyone with a single figure handicap is considered a good player. During the five weeks we played at Churston, which is just around the bay from Paignton. I bought my first set of woods from the pro there; they were Wilson Staff, quality stuff in those days! Con was always very encouraging and helped me a lot with the basics of the game.

A happy occasion which occurred during the last week of our short season was that Con had a call to say that his wife Kay had given birth to a baby boy, Philip, and after the show that evening he and I left the theatre and drove all the way to Halifax in his Roller. I went along to help with the driving, and having seen the new offspring, we drove back the next day in time for the show in the evening. With the state of the roads today, I doubt that this would now be possible. Four days later Pat came down in her new car, to move into the house that Cool Breeze were renting for their season, which followed ours, and brought Kay along with her little bundle. That little bundle is now six-feet-three and is a top-notch sound engineer, working for, amongst others, Billy Pierce.

A funny incident happened that week after Pat had arrived; she was visiting backstage and Gordon Peters had his dog with him, and just as he was due to go on for his spot the dog somehow managed to escape from the dressing room and came downstairs; in a bit of a flap, he asked Pat to take the dog – an Afghan Hound – up to his room, so up she went and just as she opened the door, the dog reared up and dashed down and onto the stage. The audience laughed and Gordon told the dog sit and lie down; it did and he got wonderful applause at the end of his act. I told him he should keep it in!

After finishing the season we did a series of midnight cabarets on the *Butlins* circuit; this was for three performances a week in various camps. As the Tommy Steele Show had followed us into the Festival, I based myself with Pat and the girls in Torquay for the rest of that season.

At the end of the Tommy Steele season Cool Breeze came to an end. They had been very successful over the past ten years with TV, records, concerts, song festivals and theatre appearances but Rosemary, who had married hotelier Philip Kendrick, in 1976, was now pregnant so things came to a natural end.

During the summer, Pat had been working on a solo act with the help of Lennie Bennett and I arranged all the music. We decided to change her name to Patti, and Dorothy Solomon suggested that the surname should be a colour. The name Gold was chosen by Patti herself, reasoning that gold was the richest colour of all! Patti Gold made her first solo appearance on the Torbay Midnight Matinee of '77, and Lennie Bennett gave up some of his allotted time for this to take place. Knowing the size of egos in show business, I can't think of many who would have done this.

She appeared on stage in a long glamorous dress and sang a very 'twee' version of *I Feel Pretty*, and then in the instrumental chorus, she lifted her dress to dance and the audience rolled with laughter because she was wearing wellies. She was a success! Wendy went into acting and musicals and had great success playing the part of Sheila in *A Chorus Line* at the Theatre Royal, Drury Lane. She is now in management and one of her famous clients is Louise Redknapp.

In late September we did two weeks of one night stands in Scotland. The Bachelors used to do a few gigs up there at the end of every summer season. It was really an excuse to play some golf, which was OK by me. We took Gary Husband to play drums. He was a teenager at the time and went on to make a name for himself in the jazz world as a pianist, drummer and composer; a right clever Dick! I bet he's never told his jazz pals that he has played for the Bachelors! Garry is from Leeds and his father Peter was a good friend of mine; he was a flautist with the *NDO*, and he used to play percussion for us when we augmented the band at Batley.

I was now getting to grips with the golf and was becoming quite dangerous off my high handicap. We were staying in a house in Falkirk that was owned by Duncan Frazer, the promoter of our short tour. He used it to put up all the acts he brought up from England. We had a bedroom each and a communal kitchen so we were able to look after ourselves; in jest, we called it the 'Falkirk Hilton'.

Falkirk, being half way between Glasgow and Edinborough

was an ideal place to stay; it was also close to Grangemouth where John Black, the golf pro was based and he took us to St. Andrews, where, after the game we were invited to have tea and sandwiches in the trophy room with Keith McKenzie, who was then the secretary of the Royal and Ancient Golf Club; probably the highest official in world golf.

On the middle Saturday of our two weeks, we played the Caledonian Hotel in Inverness. Con and I, who were travelling together, we usually did because we lived close to each other, decided that as we didn't have a gig on the Sunday, we would call at Gleneagles on the way back to Falkirk. We arrived at about one-thirty in the afternoon and it was pouring with rain. When we turned up at the pro's shop there was no chance of any golf, but being famous has its advantages, so the assistant professional who was on duty said; "Go up to the Dormy house and have a cup of tea, and if it is going to stop, it will be in the next half hour".

We went and had our tea, and we were obviously in the Lord's good books that day because it stopped raining, so we went back to the pro's shop. By now, it was three- thirty and the young pro took us down to the starter, who looked at the time and said "You will probably only be able to get nine holes in, so how does a pound apiece sound". To us it sounded fine, bearing in mind that the normal price in those days was twenty-five pounds. I think today it is ONE HUNDRED and twenty five pounds!

When I tell you that we played the King's Course, off the back tees, all eighteen holes, and we were the only two players on the course, you will realize that it was one of the greatest bargains of all time. As we played up the seventh fairway, the evening sun was shining, diamond like droplets of rain sparkled on the grass, a pheasant ran in front of us and I turned to Con and said; "I think I've died and gone to heaven". This really was millionaire's golf!

In the autumn I did the London Palladium with Pat O'Hare. Pat had won some rounds of *New Faces* and through this he had been invited by Dorothy Squires to appear on one of her Palladium concerts that she did on a regular basis around about this time. I had done about four arrangements for a thirty-piece orchestra but unfortunately she had taken up all the time in the afternoon for her own band call, this meant that we didn't get one. When new arrangements are played it is not unusual for there to be copying mistakes on the first time of playing, however, Pat went on stage without having had a call and the orchestra sight read the parts and luckily it all went fine. But such things are not to be recommended!

In October Patti made her solo debut; this was at the Sulem Voe oil refinery club in the Shetland Isles. She was picked up in Manchester by Wee Willie Harris and his band, travelling in their van to Glasgow from where they flew to the Shetlands. I was waiting at home for the call to hear how the show had gone; I had sent a large bouquet and a telegram saying "Good Luck darling, be great" etc. then the 'phone rang; "I want to come home," said this tearful voice.

"Why what's the matter love?" said I.

"While I was on stage a big oil worker said, holding a bottle, "If ya dinna sing any Scottish songs, this is goin' o'er yer heed."

Apparently, a fight then broke out and she was lifted into a corner by two heavy bouncers who stood guard to protect her. Not the best way to start a new solo career!

~*~

Over Christmas and the New Year we did a variety show at the Kings Hall in Blackburn. One of the support acts on the bill was the Mistins; a French man and his wife who played xylophones, one of which – his - was on castors. The climax of the act consisted of him putting on roller skates, and putting on a harness and fixing it to the xylophone. His wife then took up a baton and conducted the band playing *Orpheus in the Underworld* but only for show. As the band played the music at an ever increasing tempo, he started to spin himself and the xylophone around. It was a very good act, but when I recall it I smile to myself, because one time when they played a season at Blackpool Opera House, the band actually followed her direction and the whole thing collapsed in chaos!

Chapter Fourteen

My First Visit To Oz

In the early part of '78 Pat did the odd gig in places where she had worked with Cool Breeze but things weren't going too well for her. Club and theatre owners had promised her work when she went solo, but it was a culture shock for her. Whereas before she was treated with respect as a top of the bill artiste, with the number one dressing room etc, she was now back to being a support act which was like starting all over again, and being on the road on her own, after the company of the other two girls, she was lonely.

At Easter The Bachelors and Patti were booked at the Batley Variety Club and I directed for them both. Prior to this booking Patti had asked Dorothy Solomon to release her from her contract as things didn't appear to be working out as well as they might. Dorothy agreed, but sent her assistant, Lorna Davies, to see Pat during that week to try to persuade her to change her mind, but she was adamant that it was for the best.

It was a good week, but in many ways it was a sad week,

because shortly after this the club closed and Batley Variety Club was no more. I suppose there was a slight irony in the fact that we, The Bachelors, Patti and I, had been there more or less from the start, exactly eleven years - 1967 to 1978 - and now we were here at the end!

After this, Bernard Hinchcliffe became Patti's manager and agent, and within a week he had filled her book with work, including a summer season in Cleethorpes with Charlie Williams.

In May I did a *Royal Command Show* with The Bachelors at the Fairfield Hall in Croydon, in the presence of HRH Princess Anne. The show also included Vince Hill and Irish comedian Pat Mooney. After the show I, along with the cast, was presented to the Princess.

Fairfield Hall, Croydon. The Bachelors waiting to be introduced to Princess Anne.
That's me on the right doing an impersonation of her brother Charles.

I spent the summer season in Blackpool conducting the show at the ABC Theatre; again it was with The Bachelors and Billy Dainty. This time we had with us a brilliant American juggler called Dick Franco, The Mosaics, comedian Joe Church, and the Nolan Sisters. This was just before they had their recording success. Their arrangements had been done by Alyn Ainsworth and were very good, as was their singing, particularly their harmonies on *How Deep is Your Love*.

It was a very good season, the show was good, the business was good, the band was good, and the golf was good! We played at St Ann's Old Links which was an affiliated course of the Vaudeville Golfing Society (VGS) of which I had become a member. Being in Blackpool for twenty weeks was great for my handicap; I was playing every day and I came down from twenty-four to sixteen in that time. I played a lot with an American juggler called Gill Dover who was working at the Opera House. Gill was also a member of the VGS.

One evening during the finale The Bachelors presented me with a bandits mask on stage. For anyone who doesn't understand the significance of this, it is when high handicap golfers start winning everything, they are then regarded by other golfers as "bandits", because they play much better than their handicap suggests. This is something that happens when a new player starts getting to be a better player. That is the time to enjoy it, because sooner or later reality sets in and the improvement comes to a stop! During my golfing career I did manage to get down to eight, but now as I get older I seem to be settled at a respectable thirteen. But on occasions it's more like twenty!

In the first part of the season I did the Opera House concerts as usual, but Tommy Steele went in for about eight Sundays in the middle, and of course he had his own MD, Alan Bence. After this I took over again and ended the season with the normal format of a different show every week. The good thing about having the eight weeks off meant that Patti and I were able to see each other each weekend.

In early '79 I went with The Bachelors to Australia and we were there for five weeks. We went by British Airways, first class. I'd never flown first class before. Wow, it's another world! From the first class lounge at Heathrow to disembarking in Sydney it was wonderful. On entering the plane there were cigars waiting for us with the champagne, and wardrobes to hang our clothes, to allow us to change into something more comfortable. The meals were excellent and the upper deck was a bar, not like today, having been filled with seats in some cases. We stopped en route at Bombay and Bangkok, taking twenty-two and a half hours from  London to Sydney. We flew in over the city, and seeing the famous Harbour Bridge and the Opera House for the first time was a wonderful sight.

The first two weeks we worked at the South Sydney Juniors Club. A lot of these clubs in and around Sydney were attached to rugby league clubs and they were all as big – in some cases bigger and plusher – as the theatre clubs in the UK. This one was huge, with the reception and a health club with a swimming pool on the ground floor. Taking the escalator to the second floor brought us to the gaming room which was filled with "pokies"; these were the hundreds of slot machines which generated all the cash that paid for all the international stars who appeared there.

The Show Lounge was on the third floor and had all the latest theatre technology and a twelve piece band made up of some of Australia's finest musicians, who during the day, did the recording and TV sessions. The next floor had three restaurants, one was a Smorgasbord, another Chinese, and the other an ordinary Australian. On the top floor were a couple of bars, a general one with an endless supply of the amber nectar and the piano lounge for the more sophisticated, with a wonderful view, especially at night. You could see all the lights of the city and watch the planes landing at the Kingsford Smith Airport.

After these two weeks at South Sydney Juniors we did a few one nighters on the RSL circuit; these are the Return Servicemen's Legion Clubs which are the equivalent of our British Legion Clubs. These were situated in the city and the suburbs. On one occasion we went up to Newcastle, which is about a hundred and twenty miles up the coast, and there I met Pat's cousin Paul who had emigrated about nine years earlier. This was the first time we had met since then.

In the fourth week we went out into the bush, playing places in the New South Wales hinterland. Places with names like Dubbo, Orange, Parkes, Forbes and Cowra.

We went by car but returned to Sydney by plane. On our return we met up again with the Irish rugby team, who by coincidence were playing in Sydney at the same time as we were there. They had also been in Dubbo at the same time as us, staying in the same hotel, and we had become quite friendly.

I got to know the manager Noel Murphy who gave me a shamrock badge and made me an "honorary Irishman" because of my Bachelors connections! The team invited us to the test match at the Sydney Show Ground which they won. The Irish were a good team at that time with good players such as Ollie Campbell, Tony Ward and Willie John McBride.

Our base for this tour was the Sebel Town House Hotel in Kings Cross. This was in the bohemian part of the city, with night clubs and excellent restaurants; I remember in the 50's when Ted Heath and the band did a tour of Australia, Kenny Graham wrote a suite especially for it, and one of the movements was called *Kings Cross Climax*; a drum feature for Ronnie Verrel. On our first night there, we went "up the cross" for a drink. There in a small bar was a guy playing piano, and he was using an electric drum machine attachment. I smiled, and pointed out to the lads the irony of it, because on the piano was a Musicians Union sticker, on which was printed "Keep Music Live"!

While in Sydney we were invited to a few 'barbies' by several people, one of whom was Peter Coleville an English comedian who lived in Sydney. It turned out that I knew his son Robin who just happens to be one of the Grumbleweeds. Also at this barbecue were Frankie Vaughan, his pianist Phil Phillips and his drummer Kenny Hebden from Leeds, who is a friend of mine. Rolf Harris was also there, along with a few Aussie "turns" whom we had just met. Rolf was working at the St.George's Club and Frank was doing one nighters, like us.

In our last week we went to Canberra and did four shows there. It is a strange city; very symmetrical, all the roads are straight, and the lakes are all man made and they all look perfect. It is very clean and all the lawns are beautifully manicured, but everything looks very contrived.

When we arrived back in Sydney we went to the Regent Theatre to see Danny La Rue and afterwards we went to his dressing room for a drink. We were made very welcome. The Bachelors are fellow "Water Rats" and I had worked with him many times before. Another person on the show was Wayne King, a pianist whom I had conducted for many times at Blackpool Opera House. There were quite a few people in the room drinking and chatting. I was talking to a very tall good looking blonde, and after a while Con drew me to one side and whispered, "Look at the hands", I did, and thought that these hands were more suited to number eight shovels rather than embroidery needles! I looked around and realised that most of these 'women' were, in fact, transvestites!

Two days before we left for home Jeanette Peters had arrived at the hotel with The Two Ronnies, who were taking over from Danny La Rue at the Regent. They were to be in Australia for a year doing the show for the Fielding Office, which they had presented at the London Palladium.

The Sebel Town House, at the time, was one of the top hotels in Sydney, and all the big name stars stayed there. Frank Sinatra stayed there and Barry Manilow had left the week before we arrived, John Cleese stayed a few days while we were there, as did Lauren Bacall, the group 'Smokie', and Frankie Howerd. One Saturday afternoon it was raining and Frankie, Con, Dec and I went in the car, which was provided by the promoters, to Bondi Beach and parked on the headland overlooking the bay, where we just watched the surf rolling in to pass the time away. Frankie was telling us about his childhood and his career. It was very interesting but I got the impression that he was a very sad and lonely man.

This was my first visit to Australia, which I loved, but I'm happy to say it wasn't my last. I've been many times since, and hope to go again.

Chapter Fifteen

My Last Season With The Irish Lads

Quite a lot had happened while we had been away in Australia; petrol had reached a pound per gallon and Margaret Thatcher had become Prime Minister. Two major events that still have an impact, even to this day.

After dropping off my luggage at home, I went to the Isle of Man for Patti's opening night at the Villiers Hotel, where she was starring in the show for the '79 summer season along with Vince Earl.

Bernard Hinchcliffe and his wife Sheila also came over for the opening and the three of us stayed with Patti at a cottage she had rented for the season. It was after midnight when we returned to the cottage after the opening night's show, and when we switched the lights on in the kitchen a few snails were to be found on the stone flagged floor – after all it was in the countryside; thereafter Bernard always referred to the house as 'Slug Villa'.

I returned home for a few days and then I was off to Great Yarmouth to conduct what was to be my last summer season with

The Bachelors. We opened at the ABC Theatre in June with the same show that had been in Blackpool the previous year, except that the Nolan's had been replaced by 'Beverley Rainbow' and Joe Church by a young man I had never heard of: Michael Barrymore.

This is the person who, in the 90's, became one of the biggest names on television, and for the life of me I will never understand why – I was going to say "how or why"

Beverley Rainbow
Great Yarmouth 1979

but I do know how! The Bachelors Show was his first major summer season; before this he had done holiday camps. He struggled throughout the whole run and walked off the stage to the sound of his own feet after every performance, because I'm afraid he wasn't very funny.

On a personal level he was pleasant enough, and his wife Cheryl was a very nice girl. They didn't mix with the rest of the company very much, keeping themselves to themselves. That year the *Daily Mirror* did a series of features on various summer shows throughout the country, and one of the editions was about young comics. Michael didn't come out of it very well and took a huge slating from the report. Even before this, Delfont's, the promoters, kept sending some of their directors up to Great Yarmouth to monitor how he was doing and tried to persuade his management to take him off the show, but they would not agree to it.

Beverley Rainbow wasn't a girl singer, they were a three girl vocal group and they happened to be the daughters of the Beverley Sisters, hence the name. They were very young at this time in what was their first number one summer show; working for the Delfont's was a 'big deal'. They were good looking girls and they sang very well. The Beverley sisters came to visit quite a lot during the run, and Joy's husband, Billy Wright, used to come with them. Billy and I had a mutual friend in Pat O'Hare, and I very much enjoyed his company; he was actually one of my heros! After a few years of being Beverley Rainbow the girls eventually changed their name to Little Foxes. The Mosaics UV puppet act completed the bill

During rehearsals, Dickie Hurran the producer was marking out the stage settings for Billy Dainty's props table. I just happened to say that it was on stage left and Dickie insisted it was stage right. I pointed out that it was in this certain position because he went to pick up a hat after finishing by the table after a particular routine, but Dickie wouldn't have it. This man was of the old school of producers – you know, the ones with the overcoat draped over the shoulders with the velvet collar - and they are always right!

Meanwhile Billy was in the wings laughing his socks off. He knew I was right but just left me to dig a bigger and deeper hole for myself. Afterwards I said to him "You bastard Dainty", and all he did was fall about with laughter. I did three summer seasons with Billy and several concerts at Blackpool Opera House. We became good friends. I was very sad when he died of cancer at a relatively young age.

During this season the relationship between The Bachelors

themselves became very strained. This was the start of what eventually led to their break up. John and Dec stopped speaking to each other and Con, being Dec's brother, was caught in the middle; I was also in the same situation to a certain extent, but without any blood ties.

I think some of the problems were due to the fact that Dec wanted to do more contemporary material but John was content to do the stuff that they were well known for. I had arranged a lot of new numbers for this season, which were not really the type associated with the Bachelors; obscure songs such as Billy Joel's *Italian Restaurant* and a couple of reggae type numbers.

After opening night Dorothy Solomon went ballistic, pointing out that the fans expected all their favourites and that the reviews would more than likely be a disaster; she was right! The next night the new stuff was out and the old was back in. Just a couple of the new things survived and everyone (maybe Dec with reservations) was happy. I was certainly happy; I had arranged a whole new act and had been paid for it!

Again the band was on stage, the same as Blackpool, but this time we only had one trombone, Andy Crompton from Manchester, a very good player. I had taken Ken Newton on drums, Jeff Loriman on bass and trumpeter Allan Cross with me, but the rest of the band were booked by the Delfont music department and I had only known Pete Carter, the guitarist, before this.

In August '79 my hero Stan Kenton died, and in that evening's performance, I wore a black tie as a mark of respect. Joy and Billy were there that evening and they thought that it was a very nice gesture. So did I!

At the end of the season I left The Bachelors to work full time as Patti's MD. Bernard Hinchcliffe said he could get enough work for us, and at the right price. This meant we no longer met for one night at the weekends, then said goodbye for another week, and so on and so on.

I had been working on and off (mostly on) with The Bachelors since 1973 and in many ways I was sad to leave them. These were people who had had more than twenty five world-wide hits in their career and sold millions of records, including *Charmaine, Diane, I Believe, and I Wouldn't Trade You for the World.* When *Diane* was number two in the charts, they were selling ninety thousand records a day! That's a lot of records, I believe you make the charts today if you sell five thousand in a week! Some difference, eh? Through working with them I had travelled the world, I had conducted some big orchestras, I had done TV, I had conducted number one shows, played the biggest of theatres, and I had learned to play golf (allegedly!) and we are still good friends. I still see quite a lot of Con as we live close to each other and we both play golf on the Celebrity Golf Tour.

Then, came a new decade. Could it be half as good as the last? Mmm, well, maybe. We shall see!

Chapter Sixteen

A New Decade - A New Direction

Bernard was as good as his word, he did fill the book with good work, and 1980 turned out to be quite a year: Patti and I got married. After a busy spring doing the rounds we opened in Scarborough for the summer season show at the Opera House Theatre. This was topped by the Grumbleweeds, with Stu Francis, the comedian, Terry Hall, the ventriloquist, with Lenny the Lion, a comedy multi-instrumentalist called Humphrey Bunn, six girl dancers and Patti. I was the MD with a five-piece band in the pit.

Weather-wise it was awful for the first five weeks of the run, but it brought in the crowds. Don Robinson owned the theatre; the show was presented by McLeod Holden Ltd and produced by Geoff Barry. It was a fun show. Let's face it, it could hardly be anything else if the Grumbleweeds were involved. It was a laugh from start to finish.

After work we often went to Scalby Manor Hotel to relax. This was the meeting place where all the people from the shows met after the evening's performances. Peters and Lee, Janet Brown, and Roy Walker were at the Floral Hall. The original

Black and White Minstrels were at the Futurist and socially the season was excellent throughout.

The big event took place in July, what a week that was. In the lead up to the wedding, the 'weeds' and the cast had been threatening that all sorts of things were going to happen to me on my bachelor's night 'do'. According to them, I would be legless for the 'Big Day'. In fact it was just the opposite; they were all legless and I was the one left standing! I don't understand how this happened because I'm not such a big drinker.

The lads' night out took place on the Monday. The girls had their night on the Tuesday before the wedding on the Wednesday.

Bernard was my best man and Wendy, our friend from Cool Breeze, was Patti's bridesmaid. Katie, Patti's two year old niece – the reason for the Cool Breeze split – was her page girl. The night before the wedding I stayed with Edwin Heath, the hypnotist, and his wife Margaret. Edwin was doing the midnight show at the Opera House every evening after our two shows had finished.

The ceremony took place at Scarborough Register Office. Brian Shipley and his wife Mavis, the owners of Scalby Manor, provided a horse and carriage to take us through the streets to the hotel where the guests, including the cast, Charlie Williams, who was appearing down the road in Bridlington, Leon Fisk, then a 'Dallas Boy', now an agent, Roy Walker, Pat's Mum and Dad, her sister Rosemary with her husband Philip, my mother, and all our relatives and friends were waiting. There was a clip of us being transported through the crowds on the local YTV six o'clock news programme *Calendar*, and Robin, one of the 'weeds' videoed the whole day for us.

The whole day was a riot, and we finished it off by doing the usual two shows, with all the guests attending one or the other and Patti finished off the proceedings wearing her wedding dress in the finale!

Most of the social activity that season took place at the Manor and Brian and Mavis were perfect hosts. Towards the end of the season a few of the local regulars who were to be found at most of these 'dos', namely Michael Corrigan, Carl Towle, Ken Middleton and Don Robinson, booked a whole carriage for a day trip on the North Yorkshire Moors Railway from Pickering to Grossmont. This was as a thank you to all the artistes who had given them such a good time all season.

They provided smoked trout from the trout farm which is adjacent to Pickering Station, fresh salad and champagne, all in cool boxes. We left Pickering at nine in the morning; the journey took an hour and after a walk around Grosmont we retired to the pub, then on the way back we got stuck in to the trout, salad and champers. We all arrived back at the theatre for the first show at six ten.

Terry Hall, who for the previous two years had been caring for his wife who was suffering from cancer and had unfortunately died, was doing his first season for quite a few years, and to be perfectly honest he did struggle a bit. Ok when someone hasn't worked for a couple of years they are bound to be a bit rusty. This particular evening's shows were different; you see, Terry wasn't a drinker, but he had been persuaded to have a drop of champagne on the way back and that evening he did the best two shows of his life!

The Grumbleweeds were doing their very successful radio series at this time and were very popular. There was always something happening, either on stage or off. As individuals they all had something to offer: Robin was a great mimic, Graham was just a naturally funny person, Maurice was a good 'front man', Carl was very creative, he invented the character, Wilf 'Gasmask' Grimshaw and his brother Albert was the main singer in the group.

It was during this season that Stu Francis got to know that he had been picked to present *Crackerjack.* We were all very sad when the season ended, but we made friendships which have endured.

During the run Bernard brought a few TV producers to see the shows, and one in particular, John Kay Cooper, offered Patti a spot on *Search for a Star* a new talent show he was producing for LWT. She did this after the season finished in October and although she didn't win, it opened the door to more work on television. Cooper himself booked her to appear in *The Madhouse* series with Russ Abbot which ran for eight shows and after that Alan Boyd, another LWT producer booked her for twelve shows in the first series of *Punchlines* with Lennie Bennett.

Search for a Star was done in the October at the end of the season and after that she started recording *Punchlines*. She had known Lennie since the days at Batley and, as I said earlier, they did the '77 season together in Paignton. Lennie was the host and presenter of the show and Patti was one of a team of newcomers to TV who sat in boxes, and each had a punch line, one of which tagged a phrase that the two contestants were given. After the team were given their lines they were moved around the boxes to sit in another place; likened to shuffling a pack of cards, and the two guests would pick one of the team to deliver their phrase which more often than not was incorrect but would fit, with a humorous connotation.

Along with Patti the team included Roger Kitter, Fogwell Flax, Mathew Kelly, Judy Gridley and Bryan Joan Elliot. This first series featured these unknown artistes to see if the programme format would work; it did, so the following series also featured well-known guests.

These shows went out every Saturday in the first twelve weeks of 1981 at the prime time of six-thirty in the evening. After this eight weeks of *The Madhouse* followed on, meaning that Patti was on TV on consecutive Saturdays for the first twenty weeks of the year. She got a lot of good publicity, with features in national newspapers and magazines. Unfortunately this didn't go down very well with Russ Abbott. He was very jealous if he thought someone was getting more publicity than he was, which is very silly really because if a show gets good publicity it always reflects on whoever is the top of the bill.

One article in particular appeared in *The Sun* newspaper, written by Margaret Forward, and was very complimentary, and he got the 'needle' at it. John Kay Cooper, the producer, took Pat out to dinner one evening, when they were filming the '81 Christmas show, in order to break the news that Abbott had told his manager to tell him, "Get rid of her, she's too funny" and, as Abbott was top of the bill, he had no alternative but to comply. It broke her heart for a while but she was resilient and she got stuck into other things. People think Mr Abbott is a nice guy, but in our household we have other opinions.

Lennie Bennett had no such insecurities; he insisted that she did at least four shows in every subsequent *Punchlines* series. In fact she appeared in more of these shows than anyone, apart from Lennie himself.

I, personally, am not very enamoured with some of these TV executive types, they can make or break a career on a whim. The head of light entertainment at LWT was a guy called David Bell, who was gay, and he said to Patti "if I can have him", (meaning me), "I'll make you a big star". I guess I don't have to tell you my feelings on this!

During the time that Patti was doing a lot of recording for LWT we moved house from Rothwell to Tingley. The move took place one snowy January morning in 1981. Patti had gone off to London to record a couple of *Punchlines*, having left our home in Rothwell, she then returned in the early hours of the next morning to our new place in Tingley. It took her quite a while to settle in the new house and we believe that was because she never actually moved in with her belongings. I think she must have got over it by now though, twenty-five years later we are still here!

In the spring Don Robinson sent for me to go see him in Scarborough. I thought he wanted to talk about the summer season ahead, which I was due to MD for him, but when I got there he threw a bunch of keys at me and said "You didn't have a honeymoon so go and use my condo in Fort Lauderdale". We took him up on the offer when Patti finished recording all her TV shows. While there, we met Pearl Carr and Teddy Johnson who were staying in Ernie Wise's place in the same International Village; we had met them originally at Terry Hall's wedding to Denise, his second wife. We spent the week together and had a lovely time.

Chapter Seventeen

Blackpool Opera House – The End Of An Era

1981 turned out to be another good year for us, with Patti being on TV every week her profile rose considerably. After the LWT work came appearances on YTV's *3.2.1.* booked by their then casting director Linda Kramer. Linda had followed Pat's career and her rise as a solo artiste and now had something to offer her. This was when I met up again with Ted Rogers, and as before, he remembered me straightaway as if he had seen me yesterday.

The first *3.2.1.* that Patti did was with Frankie Vaughan, she played the character of a housewife who had won a night out with Frankie. In the next one she played a bank teller to Johnny More's 'Kojak' and Mike Newman was a bungling bank robber. After that she did the Christmas edition with Joan Simms who played the part of Mother Christmas. The camera focused on a dolly in Santa's Grotto, and then the dolly, played by Patti, came to life and sang and danced to a song that I and Laurie Holloway had written the music for.

Later on she did a few *Starburst* shows for Central TV. This was in the days when there was a lot of variety on television.

In between Pat's TV work, summer seasons and pantomimes, there were some very good dates in some very good venues, such as Blazers Club in Windsor, Talk of the North in Manchester, Caesar's Palace, Luton, Jollees, Stoke and the Night Out in Birmingham. We did a one nighter with Victor Borge at the Night Out and he was brilliant. The club is big and the audience sits at tables which are tiered to the back of the room and the entrance is similar to walking into a football stand with the patrons sitting below to each side and above where everyone walks in.

With Victor Borge on Canberra

I describe the layout because when Victor Borge did his spot a lady got up from her seat and made her way to the entrance and was in full view of everyone; at this point Mr Borge stopped playing and asked her if she really had to go, embarrassed, she said yes, so he said "We'll wait". He put the piano lid down, turned to face the audience, crossed his legs, looked around the room, looked at his nails, and as this was taking place a rumble of laughter started and built up to a crescendo, until everyone was laughing. As the lady came back to her seat looking very embarrassed, it must have been at least four minutes, Victor enquired of her, "OK?" She said, "Yes" and he said "I'll continue" and picked up the music half way through the bar exactly where he had stopped and the audience went wild. From a musical point of view this was brilliant.

In the summer we had a house in Muston near Filey, which was very convenient because come evening time Pat would go off to Bridlington to appear with Les Dawson at the Spa Theatre, and I would go the other way, up to Scarborough where I was leading the band at the Opera House for the show which featured the Black Abbots, Stan Boardman, Al Dean and the Minting Sisters vocal group. John Redgrave was the producer, - who everybody raves about for his lighting - well, I take issue with that, I don't think he is all that good, because he finished every scene with a black-out, and if ever there was such a thing as an applause killer, a black-out is it, and the one thing that artiste's need is applause!

During the season I had kept doing my Sunday concerts at Blackpool Opera House. As I mentioned earlier I had been doing these since 1971 and I had learned a lot about conducting in that time. From the band call at two-thirty in the afternoon I enjoyed every minute of it up to the closing at ten-twenty - except when Ken Dodd was on, we finished on a Monday!

There was a feeling of real show business about these performances. We had some great stars on the shows including Jimmy Tarbuck and Kenny Lynch, Max Bygraves, Vince Hill, Moira Anderson, Billy Dainty, Val Dooican, Lena Zavaroni, Kathy Kirby, Charlie Williams, Mike Yarwood, Les Dawson and many, many more, oh, and Patti Gold!

I also had some good musicians in the orchestra including trumpeter Johnny Brown, a good player I had known for a long time, pianist Brian Pendleton, who is also a very good arranger and was the original pianist/arranger for the *Sid Lawrence Orchestra,* Ray Barlow played bass, Jack Chadwick, Les Beavers or Dave Tanner were on guitar and dear old Al Wood was one of the regular sax players.

During the summer I had a season's membership at Scarborough South Cliff Golf Club, where the season before, the showbiz fraternity had inaugurated a trophy to be played for between the club and entertainers who were doing seasons in the resort. I don't know whether this still takes place but it did go on for quite a few years.

At Christmas Pat was principal boy in *Dick Whittington* at the Davenport Theatre, Stockport with Les Dawson and Roy Barrowclough. Meanwhile I was MD for Freddie Davies at Middleton near Manchester, who was producing *Aladdin* starring an act called Cheese and Onion; never heard of them? They won *New Faces* and after this sank without trace! I still see Barry occasionally on the Celebrity Golf Tour; he was the 'Cheese', but he is now without the Onion!

In the early part of 1982 we worked at the Dubai Marine Hotel for five weeks. This was a very enjoyable booking. The compere was J.J.Stewart, who sang, told a few gags, and played trumpet. His real name is Bob Harrison and at the time he lived in Bournemouth, but was out there doing a six-month contract. We became good friends with JJ and worked with him a few times after this.

We made friends with a lot of the patrons, the ex pats and the rich Arabs. During the day we were members of the Inter Continental Leisure Club with all its facilities, the gym, the pool, and the bars. When the sun went down in early evening we often went across the creek on a dhow – these are the boats which ply up and down the Gulf – to the shops and the gold souks. Friday, being the Muslim holy day, we didn't work, so we usually went out to one of the fabulous beaches such as Chicago or Jebal Ali, where we would fish, and anything we caught we barbequed it there and then on the beach. We couldn't do that now because this is where the famous hotels are that you see in all the travel brochures.

One Saturday afternoon it was the FA Cup Final between Spurs and Manchester City; we received this on TV and in those days there were no satellite links, so pictures and sound were fed on separate lines. After the match, which Spurs won, John Motson was going on and on about what was happening, and apparently David Coleman, the anchor man in the studio, should have been talking at this point, and he was getting very frustrated at not being able to get in to speak, so we heard Coleman sounding off to the producer "What the hell is that f—ing Motson going on about?" Not knowing that everybody in the world, apart from viewers in the UK, was hearing this. Since then, in our household, John Motson has been known as "That f—ing Motson"!

The week after this there was an England match on TV and I drew Paul Mariner in the hotel sweep for who would score the first goal; he did, and I treated myself to a Raymond Weil watch with my two hundred pound winnings. It was about sixty per cent cheaper than at home. It is still ticking away quite happily!

After Dubai we spent the summer doing various one nighters and the odd week here and there. Pat did a series of Sunday shows at the 'Three B's' theatre club in Bridlington and I did what was to be the last season of *Harold Fielding Presents* Sunday concerts at Blackpool Opera House after thirty-two years. I was sad when these finished, it was the end of an era.

The summer of '83 turned out to be quite hectic, with Pat

being on TV a lot she was in demand for various things, personal appearances, judging talent shows and beauty contests, as well as doing her stage shows. We did ten weeks of the summer doing Monday, Tuesday and Wednesday for Ladbrokes in Great Yarmouth, Thursday, Friday and Saturday at the Morecambe Bowl with her own show, and Sundays at the North Pier, Blackpool with Bob Carolgees and 'Spit the Dog'. We'd first met Bob on a series of one-night stands in early '81, working around the Portsmouth area, and then he'd worked with Pat again in the Les Dawson season in Bridlington in that summer.

While all this was going on we had an extension built on to the back of our house and this became a new dining room. I said earlier that Pat took a while to settle in our new home and although we put it on the market we didn't really push it, but after the extension was built she was happy.

In the autumn we did a week in Jersey at the Sunshine Hotel in St Helier, also staying there were Holly Day and Cherie Roland, a couple of girl singers who were appearing at the Mediterranean Night Spot, which belonged to the same owners, and Al Showman whom we'd first met at Batley, He was a very funny comic. One morning we came down stairs and this bald fellow was brushing a wig on his knee; it was Al but at first we didn't recognise him because we never realized he was bald! I believe that shortly after that he moved to Australia.

In November I stayed with David Vicars and Richard Chandler for a week. I had first met them through Patti when they did the Tommy Steele Tour as The Mosaics; they created this act featuring giant puppets under ultra violet lighting and the effect was spectacular. They were then in the Blackpool and Great Yarmouth summer season shows with me and we had become good friends. In this week we did three shows, one in Lewisham, one in Grays and one in Maidstone.

David and Richard had created two new puppet characters; JD' and 'Ginge', a bear and a racoon and they had written a show around these two characters; a children's fantasy called *Magic Mountain* and I had written the music for it. These were the first public performances of the show and they went very well. Among the cast, playing the princess, was a teenager making her first appearance in a show as a professional, a young girl called Sally Whittaker, who is now well known as Sally Webster in *Coronation Street*.

We did the show for a week the following February in Clacton. David and Richard are very talented people. They created the fantasy ballet for the Palladium production of *Hans Christian Andersen* starring Tommy Steele. They don't perform as much these days but they are very successful producers of pantomimes.

Chapter Eighteen

Not Bad For A Circus Band!

In the summer of '84 we did a season in Jersey at Caesar's Palace for Dick Ray who also presented the show at the Opera House. Patti was the headliner and it also featured JJ Stewart, the guy we met in Dubai, a young singer from Liverpool called James Stone, who was very good and performed a lot of Michael Jackson numbers, comedian Alan Fox and six girl dancers.

It was a very spectacular show and was well produced by Dick. I even appeared in some of the production routines, playing trombone in an excerpt from *Barnum*, little did I realise at this point that I would be conducting the show in Manchester in a few months time!

Michael Crawford rehearsing for Barnum

The weather that summer was great, and Jersey is a lovely place, although there was a chickenpox epidemic on the island and I contracted shingles – not very nice! Shingles is the same virus as chickenpox and I had it around my ears and hairline. Mobile phones weren't in use then and I think I got the disease from the local telephone box through using it to keep in touch with the mainland.

The season was going great and we had nice friends in our show and other shows around the island. We had super parties and 'barbies'. Barbara Windsor and Trevor Bannister were at the opera house in a farce, Les Rawlins and Eric York were at Swanson's Hotel in *Minstrel Magic*, Barbara Law and Kenny "G" were at 'The Mediterranean' and Shane Ritchie was just starting his career in another show, and they, along with a lot of other acts, helped to make it a very happy season.

Our friends Bryan and June Auty came to stay with us for a couple of weeks. We had a lovely house in the north west of the island with the gorgeous Five Mile Road beach about a mile down the road. Pat's mum and dad also came to stay.

We opened in May, and in June I had a call from Jeanette Peters at the Harold Fielding office asking if I would be interested in conducting *Barnum* at Manchester Opera House starting in September, would I!? Just like the time I was offered Mexico, I said YES!

I had never conducted a West End show before, Ok, I'd done summer seasons, variety shows and pantos, but this was the big stuff and I wasn't about to miss it. I was about to move up to another level. The Manchester Opera House had been a bingo hall for six years and, with the success of the Manchester Palace

Theatre, the Trust which ran it decided to reopen the Opera House and they wanted a big show to open with. They asked Harold Fielding to present *Barnum*, starring Michael Crawford, as this had been a huge success at the London Palladium, having run for two years.

Mike Reed, who had been the MD for the Palladium production, was now doing other work and didn't want to be out of London for a run of six months so I was offered the MD's job. I thought that showed great loyalty to me by Jeanette Peters, because she was the one who suggested that I be offered the job and Harold agreed. After all I had done ten years for the company at Blackpool, but they were variety shows and this was a production show, so from their point of view it may have seemed a gamble because I hadn't done anything this big before, but I was confident that I could do it and that is what happened.

I left Pat in Jersey in August and stayed with our friend Wendy for four weeks during rehearsals in London. During these rehearsals I was working with Mike Reed and a rehearsal pianist getting to know the show –I even learned to juggle three balls – and then we did two weeks in Manchester before opening.

We had a good orchestra, made up of mainly *NDO* players. This pleased me because I knew them and had worked with them all before. Mike Reed and Michael Crawford were very impressed when they heard the first notes of the first band call.

The show ran for six months and was a sell out at every performance. Michael Crawford was, and is, a terrific performer but he came across to me as someone very insecure, because he needed telling how well he had done after every performance by all the sycophants he had around him. Having been on the jazz,

132

variety and big band side of the business I wasn't into all the "dahlings and lovies" of the musical theatre, never the less I enjoyed it and made some good acquaintances.

I was fortunate to have a very good band to conduct. Among the musicians were Fred Kelly and Bill Pettigrew from the *NDO* trumpet section and Dave Browning who is heard every Monday, Wednesday, Friday and Sunday on TV. It is he who plays the trumpet on the *Coronation Street* signature tune. The trombones were led by Barry Dakin and the score of *Barnum* calls for the lead trombone to play euphonium in certain parts of the show and Barry played it beautifully.

The rhythm section was made up of Pete Lingwood on percussion.I gave Peter his first professional job in the band at Bournemouth Pavilion in 1976 on piano, he's an excellent pianist. The late Bob Turner was the drummer, I couldn't have had anyone better! Les Beavers, who used to play for me at Blackpool Opera House, was on guitar and the bass player was Brian Day – one of the best, he often played for the *Stuart Atkins Orchestra.*

The show used two pianos, one in each box on either side of the proscenium arch. One pianist was Stephen Hill, he was also the rehearsal pianist and deputy MD and the other was the 'Master' – my friend Tom Steer. I said earlier, he is without doubt the best pianist I have ever been fortunate enough to work with.

In the reed section I had big Roger Fleetwood – all six feet four of him , a great tenor saxophone player Garry Cox, and Albert Wood. Albert needs a whole paragraph to himself to be able to describe his instrumental ability. I first met Albert at Wakefield Locarno Ballroom. I did a dep on trombone with Denis Langfield's band and Albert was playing tenor sax. Then he played in the

Blackpool Opera House band for me on sax, clarinet and flute. He played with the *NDO* where he filled the third/jazz chair in the trumpet section. He played bass trombone with the *Maynard Ferguson Orchestra.* He played bass for me on a Bachelors Christmas show in Blackburn. He has played trumpet and lead alto for my big band. He also plays piano. He's a right bloody 'clever dick' — but I love him! Bob Turner once threatened that if he ever saw him holding a pair of drumsticks, he would chop off his hands! That was the best circus band there ever was!

The set was like a circus ring with the band in a half circle and so that the two pianists in the boxes were synchronized with the rest of the band, the three of us were linked by headphones, and I had to count everything in. I even had a speaking part! I had to introduce 'The Swedish Nightingale' – Jenny Lind, in an American accent. I didn't miss a performance and I think the deputy MD was a bit miffed at not getting a go at waving the baton.

I had great admiration for the young kids who made up most of the cast, not only were they actors, but gymnasts as well. They used to go into the theatre at three o'clock in the afternoon to warm up their muscles and practice their balancing and juggling skills, then I would go in at about five and take them through voice warm-ups doing scales etc.

I did miss one cue in the whole six months. It was a night I was waiting for a call from Pat who had been in Scotland recording a TV show with Marian Montgomery, Lennie Bennett, Garry Wilmot, Cardew Robinson, Peter Clayton and Humphrey Lyttleton. It was very foggy and there had been a report of a plane crash and I hadn't heard from her at the arranged time so I was very worried. This caused me to miss the cue but we managed to get over it and the audience 'never saw the join'. She rang later saying they were delayed because of the fog.

I'm not really a fan of the modern stage musical – yes, I know, call me old fashioned, but I prefer the shows of Rogers and Hammerstein, Jerome Kern, Cole Porter etc. To me there doesn't seem to be enough good tunes in them. Modern writers seem to get one good tune and flog it to death throughout the show, whereas those composers I just mentioned had at least half a dozen hummable tunes in each of their shows. And a lot of these became 'standards'.

I feel the same way about the singers. They tend to be actors who sing or singers who act and consequently they turn out to be average at both. There are exceptions, Elaine Page being one and of course the greatest of them all, Streisand! The West End style of singing seems to concentrate on volume rather than tone quality and style. I believe that the truly great stars come from the other side of the business - I'm not talking about that lot from Covent Garden or 'The Met'. Artistes from the jazz and variety environment learn their trade from working in all sorts of dives and dens and become better performers through this experience, whereas in the musical theatre it seems to me that people go to stage school, learn to sing, dance and act, and then become puppets of a director. They don't get the chance to develop a stage personality of their own because they haven't 'died on their ass' a few times and been able to learn from the experience. It's not pleasant but, it works!

I'm not saying the musicals don't produce any stars, but the great ones do come from the "other side of the tracks". For instance, Sinatra. He schlepped around as a big band singer during his formative years, and being around musicians such as Tommy Dorsey and Harry James, musicianship and feeling was bound to rub off. Bassey sang in social clubs and then night clubs and believe me, that isn't easy. This is where artistes learn to communicate with their audience. In fact it is hard enough to attract their attention never mind communicate! Just watch Bassey and look into her eyes, they are alive, and yet I have seen so many theatre singers and their eyes are dead, that is the difference, and it is all due to where apprenticeships are served.

Back to Crawford; he isn't the greatest of singers but he is a fine performer – and yes, his eyes are alive – and I have a lot of respect for him, even though I do think he is, or was when I worked with him, insecure, when really and truly he has no need to be because he is very talented.

Chapter Nineteen

On Tour With Freddie And Lennie

Barnum finished in Manchester in February and shortly after Patti and I flew out to South Africa to join the QEII for a booking on the Durban to Bombay leg of the '85 world cruise. We left Heathrow on the Sunday evening and thirteen hours later landed in Johannesburg. This was in the days of apartheid and South African Airways planes were not allowed to fly over black African countries, so they had to go the long way round and more or less follow the coast around the 'bulge'. After a stopover in Johannesburg, to drop off passengers and to refuel, we flew on to Durban which only took an hour. We stayed at the Holiday Inn, on a most beautiful beach, and joined the ship on the Tuesday.

Bertice Reading was performing on the ship and she travelled with us from London. She was one of the featured artistes on the pop show *Oh Boy* and had a hit with a song called *Nick-a-Knack-a-Knock,* and though we may think that diamond encrusted nails are a modern phenomenon, she was wearing them in 1985.

Our first port of call was Mombassa in Kenya where we went with some of the ship's resident musicians who had hired a bus, on safari for the day. We saw lions and tigers along with wildebeest and springbok, and we saw red elephants. This was due to the ochre coloured dust from the earth. When we arrived at the Safari Lodge Joe Loss was there with another party, and I gave him the Sunday Times Magazine that I read on the way out, which had a feature about him and the band doing their fourteenth consecutive world cruise on the QEII. When we arrived back at the ship we were all covered in the red dust, and one of the bands had to play for a cocktail party as the ship pulled away so they had to rush to shower. When we saw them in the evening they all looked like pandas with red dust around the eyes!

Our next port of call was the Seychelles. We went in by tender after anchoring off Mahe, the capital of the main island. We saw the huge turtles – which are revered - in the main square and took a trip over the mountain to the other side of the island, and as we went over the mountain it rained, apparently it does this just for ten minutes, at the same time every day.

We next called at Karachi in Pakistan. This was the maiden voyage to Karachi and we were greeted on the quayside by bands, jugglers, streamers and dancing camels as we pulled in.

One highlight of the trip was meeting the famous pianist Maura Limpany, we had dinner with her one evening, what a charming lady she was, and a great player specializing in Beethoven and Chopin. I never missed any of her concerts.

We finished our engagement at Bombay and left the ship at midnight. We were advised to soak our hankies in perfume to alleviate the smell we would encounter on our journey to the airport. I'm glad we did, the stench was awful. As the bus drove through the city people were sleeping on the pavements, and we could see rats running in and out between the sleeping bodies.

At the airport it was chaos, taking twenty minutes to process every person. The security was so tight because this was just after the Air India jumbo jet had been blown out of the sky just off the Irish coast. We were due to leave at five a.m. but didn't get on to the plane until five-thirty, and when at last we sat in our seats Pat just burst into tears with relief due to the tension which had built up during the check in.

We hadn't been home long before we were off on our travels once again, this time it was a tour with Freddie Star and Lennie Bennett. We opened at the Blackpool Grand Theatre on Sunday and went from there to Glasgow Pavilion which was the first of a few Scottish dates taking us as far up as Aberdeen. On our way up to Scotland we called to see my friend John Black, the pro at Grangemouth Golf Club, who asked us where we were staying. We said we hadn't fixed anything yet and he said: "You're staying with me." So we went and did the show and came back to Grangemouth and stayed with him for the time we were up there.

One day we were in his shop and John put a golf club in Pat's hands and showed her how to grip it. She had a swing and she was hooked and because he wouldn't take any payment for our stay with him, we felt we owed him something, so at the end of the week we bought a set of ladies clubs from him. All these years later I wonder if it might have been cheaper to stay at the Hilton!

The band for the tour had been put together by Gerry Alison. Gerry lived in Leeds and was co-owner of 'Pop Plan', along with Alan Lowe. Pop Plan was an arranging service which provided arrangements of current tunes of the day for most of the bands on the ballroom circuits, and they could be played by any line up from a trio to a big band. They are known as stock arrangements. When I started playing in dance bands the stock arrangements were done by a fellow called Jimmy Lalley and every band in the country had a Lalley arrangement in its pad. The MD for Freddie was Eddie Peacock and I was MD for Patti and Lennie.

After the Scottish section the tour continued as far south as Cornwall where we stayed in a lovely hotel overlooking the beautiful estuary at Fowey. Patti and I did the West Country part in Lennie's car but Freddie flew in by helicopter commuting from his home in Maidenhead.

We did the Apollo Theatre in London and when we were getting ready for the show in the dressing room we heard someone shouting: "Patti Gold where are you? Come on Goldie where are you?" It was Barbara Windsor with a huge bouquet and a magnum of champagne. We had seen quite a lot of Barbara in Jersey the year before.

Lennie Bennett had a reputation of being a know-all and arrogant, in fact it was all a front. He did give that impression but in reality he would do anybody a good turn rather than a bad one. When Leon Fisk, the ex Dallas Boy who had put this tour together, was starting out in management Freddie was going through one of his low periods and it was Lennie who persuaded Leon to take a chance and sign him up, and these two, along with Max Clifford, who did the publicity for the tour, were responsible for the upturn in Freddie's career. "Freddie Starr Ate My Hamster" in *The Sun* newspaper at this time was all down to Max. One thing about Max – he gets people noticed!

Over the years Freddie Starr has been accused of all sorts of things but one thing he can't be accused of is being drunk. Freddie Starr does not touch alcohol, he is not a drinker. One thing he can be accused of is that he is a joker. One evening when Pat went on stage a pair of shoes that were there for her to change into at a point in the act were fastened together, and the stool she used for one of her numbers was on top of the piano. This would have thrown some people, but not PG (Patti Gold). When she got to the part where she used the stool she just climbed onto the piano, sat on the stool where it was, and sang the number without any reference to the situation at all. It brought the house down.

In the past a lot of female entertainers hadn't been able to cope with Freddie's antics and had finished up in tears. There was one girl who was doing a season in Great Yarmouth with him who couldn't handle him, and with the encouragement of her mother walked off the show. At the time this made all the national papers, some people will do anything for publicity! PG, however, gives as good as she gets, and he likes her for it.

Towards the end of the tour a very sad thing occurred. On Saturday May 11th we were to play the Harrogate Conference Centre and on the way to the gig I was listening on Radio Leeds, to the match featuring Huddersfield Town, when the station presenter broke into the programme and cut to the Bradford City game. This was the day of the fire which was to take many lives and cause many injuries. It was a very subdued performance that evening.

In the summer PG topped the Bill at the Spa Theatre, Bridlington. It was presented by Trafford Parnell and there were three different productions in the week. Monday and Tuesday had a World War II theme, Wednesday and Thursday was an Old Time Music Hall and Friday and Saturday was a Variety show. I wasn't involved with this because the company carried their own resident band, so Bernard fixed me a gig playing piano in the lounge bar adjacent to the theatre.

After the season ended we went back on the merry-go-round of weeks here and there at clubs and theatres around the British Isles.

The two of us!

Chapter Twenty

Uncle Frank - He's A Cracker!

In early '86 we did a trip to New York and back on the QEII. On the outward part of the trip the sea was very rough and apart from doing a couple of cabarets I spent most of the crossing in the cabin on my back – sea sickness. If you haven't had it you won't realise how much I prayed to God asking to die! It is the worst feeling in the world!

One evening the swell was so bad that all entertainment was cancelled and Edwin Heath should have been performing, but like nearly everyone else, he was also flat out. That is, apart from his wife Margaret and my wife Pat, who, I understand, were in one of the bars with no one else apart from the two barmen and, because it was very quiet, the barmen invited the two girls to help them with a bottle of brandy! While they were living it up, everyone else was lying down. The next day the sea was calmer and while everyone else was living it up, *they* were lying down!

As we approached our destination Coney Island was on our starboard (right) side and on rounding Brooklyn and going under the Verrazano Bridge we saw the famous Manhattan skyline ahead of us as we passed the Statue of Liberty. The Staten Island Ferries criss-crossed in front of us as we drew ever closer to our berth, with the imposing World Trade Centre Towers dominating everything. The whole panorama was probably the most famous in the world. How sad it is that it was altered by an act of evil treachery.

This was our first time in New York and we did the usual tourist bit as we always did. The Empire State Building, Madison Square Garden, Macey's, Time Square, the lot. It is true, New York, New York *IS* a wonderful town!

The voyage back was totally different; calm as a mill pond all the way (I must stop using these song titles!) and we met some very nice people on board. Alan King the Jewish American comedian joined us to entertain with his brand of humour, he was great. We also met Mary Cantor Baker, who happened to be the daughter of Eddie Cantor, and she took a real shine to Patti. She wanted her to go and stay with her and her husband. She said she could find work in America for her in the Catskills and Las Vegas but it just so happened that Pat was doing very nicely thank you over here at the time. In fact we had just received a cable from Bernard telling us that he had fixed a TV series for her with Jimmy Cricket. It is a great boost to the ego though when someone offers you something like that.

Another person who was very complimentary was David Suskind, the Hollywood film producer/director who told Pat that her interpretation of *Send in the Clowns* was the best he had ever heard.

Michael Barrymore was also on this trip but he never ventured out of his cabin. I think he must have been very troubled, even in those days. He 'died', or as the Yanks say – 'bombed', on every performance. They looked at him open mouthed, they couldn't understand what he was doing – but then again, neither could I. He was just as unfunny as he had been in Great Yarmouth in '79.

When we arrived home I had a call asking if I would like to play trombone on a tour that Freddie Starr was about to do. It so happened that this coincided with the time that Pat was to record the Jimmy Cricket series, so I was available. The trouble was I hadn't been 'blowing' for quite a while, so I said that if they would give me a week to see if I could get my 'chops' into shape I would give them an answer, one way or the other. I did the gig and enjoyed it, it was nice to be blowing again and one of the trumpet players was Bruce Addams, one of the best around. This was our first time of meeting but we have worked together quite a bit since.

In the summer Patti was second top to Frank Carson at the South Pier Theatre, Blackpool. Other acts in the show were a husband and wife comedy duo called Babs and Spider; a very funny act; and a tap dancing act, Kenny and Kaz, another husband and wife team. I was MD, with myself on keyboards, Peter Laird on bass and Dave Minshull on drums. It was a Bernard Hinchcliffe Presentation and was to be produced by Duggie Chapman, it actually finished up being produced by Patti Gold and Stuart Atkins!

At the first rehearsal get together the opening number was going to be *A Live Show is the Best Show.* On hearing this Patti and I blew a fuse at the thought of using this number. It was 1986 and I had done this song just after World War II in the late forties, and we insisted that there be a re-think, something more up to date. We called a meeting with Bernard and after a big row Mr.

Chapman – who is really an 'Old Time Music Hall' producer - decided to withdraw his services. It was now sink or swim, we had three days to get a show on. We had a dance troupe of twenty kids called the Coco-Tots and we used them in the opening with the song *Aggadoo*. It may have been rubbish but at least it was up to date rubbish!

After three days of hard slog we managed to put on a show, everyone got stuck in and worked their butts off. Uncle Frank (Carson) was his usual brilliant self and between us all we had a very successful season. A bonus was that Patti was being seen in the six week TV series of *And There's More* – Jimmy Cricket's catch phrase – which coincided with the show.

During this season Patti started playing golf seriously and took lesson at St.Anne's Old Links Golf Club from Gwyllam Hardiman, the professional. Gwyllam is a lovely guy and a very good teacher, and in fact her having lessons improved my golf no end!

Backstage Pat's dressing room was up a flight of steps and her door was opposite Frank's. During the run Frank had a habit of going in to her dressing room and changing the TV channel on entering. In the last week as Frank arrived before the show one evening, he threw a box into Pat's room and in mock annoyance she shouted "You change my TV programmes, you pester me when I'm putting on my make-up and now you throw me your rubbish." He said, "Open it, go on open it." Inside was a brand new Wilson Tournament golf bag with her name on it, in the same lettering as Nick Faldo who was a Wilson Player at the time. It also said on it, 'Stolen from Frank Carson'. That's why she calls him Uncle Frank!

Towards the end of the season I arranged and produced a

record for Frank at a studio in Fleetwood. We used the Coco-Tots on the backing of a couple of numbers written by Frank, one was called *It's a Cracker* (I wonder where he got that from?) and the other was called *Balbriggan* which is the name of a small town just north of Dublin, and Frank just happened to be the Mayor – this is true!

At the end of the season we were all feeling a little bit stale and Pat and I felt we needed a change of management. Bernard wasn't very happy about it but we were adamant. Someone once said: "Every now and then a horse needs a new jockey", and this was exactly how we felt. We didn't fall out with Bernard because he had been very good for us and was responsible for a lot of our successes. We did go ahead though, and changed agents – to Derek Franks.

Chapter Twenty-One

Come Fly With Me!

I had known Derek Franks since the late '60's when he and his then wife did a double act. He asked me to do some arrangements for them and over the years I got to know him reasonably well. He then became the compere at the Rainbow Club in Bradford and it was there that he met Gerry Marsden – of the 'Pacemakers', and this led to him becoming manager and agent for Gerry, who was struggling a bit at the time. By now, in 1986, he had become very successful with several other good acts on his books; these included Tony Christie and The Black Abbots besides Gerry.

After finishing the season in Blackpool, Derek fixed us a tour of Stakis Hotels taking in about thirty dates nationwide. We were performing to travel agents after they had been given a slide show and a meal, which was all part of a big Stakis promotion push for their hotels and a holiday village in Aviemore. We travelled all over the country from Aberdeen in the north to Plymouth in the south staying in some lovely hotels, which were all part of the deal.

In early December we had a commitment to Don Jones to do a Christmas Show for the troops in the Falklands. Don was JJ Stewart's agent and he had put this show together for CSE before we appointed Derek to represent us. But there were no problems with that. We had first met Don in Jersey during the '84 season, prior to him being an agent he had been a Mecca band leader, and prior to that he had been a baritone saxophone player with the *Eric Winstone, Frank Weir* and *Vic Lewis Orchestras*.

A few friends

The show comprised of Patti, JJ, a young comic called Jonathan and four girl dancers. I played keyboards with the bass and drummer I'd used in Blackpool the previous summer, Peter and Dave.

Don saw us off from Brize Norton RAF base one evening at around midnight and we flew in a RAF Tri-Star to Ascension Island where we stayed for five days to entertain the forces who were stationed there. As we approached Ascension Patti was invited into the cockpit for the landing and she asked air traffic control for permission to land. The weather was warm and we stayed in billets which were very nice. The garrison was not very big, it was just an airstrip really where they used to service and refuel the planes that were flying to the Falklands.

The terrain was very volcanic and it was here that NASA tested the moon buggy because the terrain was the nearest thing to the surface of the moon. In these rocks was a cemetery containing the remains of some of the crew of Captain Cook's ship '*Endeavour*', as they returned from their voyage to Australia. Patti and I actually played golf there, adjacent to the cemetery was a nine hole golf course – One Boat Golf Club - marked out, it had no grass, just volcanic gravel, and we had to put on 'browns', these are made of sand mixed with oil and rolled into a smooth surface. The clubs were borrowed from the NAAFI, thank the Lord for that, after playing on that surface for one round they were knackered!

After the shows on Ascension we took off for the Falklands which took about eleven hours. The Tri-Star was a very comfortable plane and like all RAF planes the seats were facing backwards. We all had plenty of room because it wasn't very full. On the way there JJ and I were writing a script for a TV game show about golf. He had been involved with a friend of his in creating another game show, so with my knowledge of golf and his experience of game show writing we had a go. When we arrived back in the UK Don got involved and we presented it to YTV, who were very interested, but unfortunately computer type games were becoming popular and this was more in the traditional style of game show. It was called *Par 4 the Course.*

Mount Pleasant, the military headquarters in the Falklands, was huge and all the buildings were linked by miles of corridors wide enough for vehicles to drive through. It was summer, which was similar to our early spring but with a constant wind, and it was very sunny. We didn't see any trees and I understand that the terrain is similar to the Shetlands. The sea was crystal clear with white sand in lovely bays. If the Falklands were in a warm part of the world it would be full of millionaires' yachts, it is so beautiful.

We were transported to various camps around the islands by

helicopter. These were usually made up of a series of containers, the sort used on ships for transporting large goods around the world, and they were arranged in the shape of H blocks and welded together. They were fitted out with rooms for officers, sleeping quarters and recreation and the whole camp could function without having to be exposed to the elements. We would do a show stay overnight in the billets, then next day the 'chopper' would arrive and take us on to our next gig. We would arrive around lunch-time and then we would go and explore the place. We saw hundreds of penguins and they were quite tame, we could get within feet of them as they sat there on their eggs.

One morning after a show on Mount Alice we were fogged in and it was a long time in clearing. The 'chopper' couldn't get in because it was considered too dangerous with the fog, so one of the vehicles, which had two wheels at the front and tank like tracks at the back, went down the track, which was about a mile and a half, and the helicopter pilot used this as a guide and followed it up to the top. As we waited in the fog we could hear this eerie sound in the distance and then rays of light appeared over the edge of the mountain followed by the rotors and finally the helicopter. It reminded us of the film *Close Encounters of the Third Kind,* and we all sang in unison:

This was the theme tune that was played in the film as the spaceship appeared. Some of the helicopters were supplied by the private company Bristow Helicopters and the soldiers nicknamed them 'Erics' after the famous darts player. I remember one journey from Goose Green we were in a big Chinook double rotor job and Pat was in the cockpit with the pilots who foolishly let her take the joystick. Bad move for us in the back because there was a spare fuel hose laid on the floor with some residual fuel in it, and the smell of that, combined with Pat's aerobatics did not help with the comfort of the passengers. I was sick!

Patti and co-pilot

We did a show for the Islanders in Port Stanley Town Hall which was very much appreciated and at the reception afterwards we were in conversation with some of the top brass, one of whom told me he had taught both Prince Charles and Prince Andrew to fly helicopters. This officer took us on a tour of the hangers which housed the Phantom bombers and we all got to sit in the cockpit. After this I think Patti expected to receive her wings!

One thing that the squaddies appreciated was the fact that there was no swearing and blue jokes in the shows, because every comic who had been before us had been blue. They said that if they wanted blue jokes and swearing they could do that themselves, and they thanked us for being clean.

On the way back we called in at Ascension again to refuel. We were away for two weeks and it was a very enjoyable experience.

A couple of months later we did another CSE tour to Northern Ireland with the same show apart from Peter Laird who was replaced by Jeff Loriman on bass. This time the tour manager was our old friend Arthur Dakin, who by this time wasn't doing so much playing and was getting into the management side of the business.

We stayed in a nice small hotel - can't get away from these bloomin' song titles – in Hillsborough on the outskirts of Belfast and we were transported to the gigs by private coach. This was because it was more dangerous in army vehicles.

Some of the shows took place at lunch time, others in the evening. One day we did four shows in three different places, we left Belfast one morning, drove to South Armagh towards Newry and arrived at Bessbrook, a mill complex which was used as a garrison. We did a show there for the troops who had just come off patrol duty and after that we were taken by helicopter to Fork Hill. The pilots stayed close to the contours of the terrain and never went the same way twice. This was so that the IRA could not plot to bring down one of these choppers, which had they done so would have been a great propaganda coup.

Fork Hill was a lookout post on the border, which was known as 'bandit country', as was our next stop - Crossmaglen. After we had done our third show in about five hours we were taken back to Bessbrook where we did our fourth and last show of the day. After that sleep came very easily and we were taken back to Hillsborough the next morning.

That evening we did a show in an Officers' Mess in the city. After the show we were having supper and chatting to officers when a 2nd Lieutenant came in and spoke confidentially to the Commanding Officer. We were ordered to finish our supper and get back on the coach. We later learned that a bomb had gone off a few streets away, and as we passed close to the action on our way back to the hotel, we saw the helicopter lights trained on to the road where this happened. I was told that these helicopters could not shine their spotlights any closer than three hundred feet because the power is so strong it would melt the tarmac.

We returned home from Northern Ireland and went on to the merry-go-round again, a week here and a week there, but come the twelfth of April we were on our way to Bahrain for a tour of the Gulf with Gerry and the Pacemakers.

We flew from Gatwick and as we were in the departure hall Howard Keel, who had been on *Live from Her Majesty's* on TV the night before, was checking in for his flight back to the States. Patti went up to him and wished him "Happy Birthday" and he said "Thank you, but how did you know it was my birthday", she told him that it happened to be my birthday and she knew that they coincided.

We arrived in Bahrain via Gulf Air, who was a part sponsor of the trip, and it was hot, naturally! Our first show was at the hotel we were staying in and the performance took place in the open air that first evening. They had a permanent stage in the garden which had a 'Hollywood Bowl' type of canopy over it plus good lighting and sound facilities. After Bahrain we flew to Muscat, capital of Oman, where during the sound check, again this was in the open air, I had my Ricoh camera stolen. I wasn't best pleased about that but I replaced it with a Pentax from the Dubai duty free shop and claimed the insurance when I arrived home.

After Muscat on to Abu Dhabi. We appeared to spend as much time in the air as on the ground!

In Abu Dhabi we stayed at the Holiday Inn and did the show there, most of the audiences were ex pat British, Australian and Americans, a lot of them working in the oil industry. Next day we went to Dubai by car. The organizer of the trip was an agent from Newcastle, called Bill Thompson, who took a lot of shows out to the Gulf. He hired three cars and I drove one of them, taking Patti, Gerry and his roadie. We drove to the Dubai Country Club where we were to perform that evening. Our journey, which was about two hundred kilometres, took us on the coast road and just before entering Dubai we passed the Emirates Golf Club site which was just being constructed.

When we arrived at the Country Club I went out for a few holes of golf – the course being on sand, you took out a mat to strike the ball off, and the putting surfaces were not 'greens' but 'browns' – it was so hot that I came in after two holes!

After the show we stayed at the Hyatt Regency Hotel and our room overlooked the racing track where the Dubai Formula One Grand Prix takes place. It is a massive hotel; just off the reception was an ice skating rink and beyond that was a large shopping mall.

The next day Bill Thompson and Gerry and the Pacemakers flew in a six seater plane to an island close to the coast of Iran. We didn't go because women weren't allowed to go there, so Patti and I, along with Andy, Gerry's PA and roadie, who stayed behind because there wasn't enough room in the plane, kept the car and drove to the Holiday Inn in Abu Dhabi to await their return. We then flew to Doha the capital of Qatar. Flying between the different Emirates we used Gulf Air 737's and the planes were nearly always empty so we had plenty of room to stretch out.

In Qatar the hotel, as always, was very opulent. We did a show there in the evening of the day we arrived and the next day we went out into the desert to set up for a show we did in a huge Bedouin tent. We went back to the hotel after setup and on returning to the tent, where we were to perform, my keyboard had warped with the heat, it was so hot. Luckily it still played but Qatar is the hottest place I have ever been to.

The next morning Patti woke up complaining of palpitations so we went down to the nurse in the clinic – all these hotels had a clinic with a resident nurse – and she gave her six salt tablets and advised her to get some Staminade – this is a powder to add to soft drinks and it is rich in salts and minerals - and if she couldn't get Staminade, drink *7Up*, because that also had salt and minerals in it. We did as the nurse advised and took it every day thereafter. In heat like it was there it is very easy to become dehydrated.

From Doha we went back to Abu Dhabi for a show at the British Club. On completing the show at eleven-thirty we dashed to the airport for the twelve-fifteen plane and flew to Sharjah arriving at twelve-forty-five. From there we took taxis to Dubai airport to await the British Caledonian flight for Hong Kong at four-thirty in the morning.

The plane arrived on time and an hour later we were on our way to Hong Kong. We slept a little on the way, although we had a few winks in Dubai airport on the lovely big settees, we weren't rested but we were able to get a few hours on route to HK.

One memory I have of flying in was how close we were to the skyscraper apartment blocks on either side of the flight path. As we approached it was tea time and we could see people sitting at their tables having their evening meals. This was before we actually touched down!

Hong Kong was notorious for the amount of time it took to get through customs, but on this occasion we were whisked through without any delay. Bill Thompson who did a lot of these tours had radioed ahead to tell them he was coming through and the show needed to be on stage at eight o'clock at the China Fleet Club. I don't know whether there were any palms greased or not but we made curtain up on time.

Half way through the act Pat turned to me as if in a trance and said: "Crikey! We're in Hong Kong", as if she couldn't believe it because we had been in a daze for the past twenty hours.

We finished our part of the show at the interval and left Gerry and his lads to finish off while we went from the club, which was on Hong Kong Island, back through the tunnel to The Holiday Inn on Kowloon side where we were staying. Waiting for us after checking in were the B Call crew who had brought us, and they had ordered a Chinese supper for us. They had brought with them all the bottles of champagne from the aircraft so we didn't get the early night we had promised ourselves!

We had arrived in HK on the Monday and we didn't have to work again until Friday, time for some serious sight seeing.

The next day we went on the famous Star Ferry across to the Island. On the other side we took a cab for a trip around the Island, passing Happy Valley Race Track, The Royal Hong Kong

Golf Club, and finishing up at Stanley Market. This was a veritable Aladdin's Cave of sequined dresses. Patti's eyes almost popped out at seeing so much glitter and, as you can imagine, the plastic took a bit of a bashing! She bought enough stage dresses for many years to come; in fact I believe she still has a couple.

Another day we set out to buy presents for the folks back home and we were going to treat ourselves to a fake Rolex apiece but we saw a real good looking Seiko in a pucker jeweller's window and I really had to have it, and have it I did. I have a thing about watches. Oh, you guessed! Do you know, I have had a Christmas card from The Regent Jewellers, where I purchased the watch, every year ever since.

One evening we went to another market which took place in a street which was closed to traffic for the duration of the market. We cajoled the 'Pacemakers' to go with us; these were young lads who spent most of their time sleeping during the day and staying up all night, but Pat pointed out to them that they were very lucky to have the opportunity to see things in the world for nothing that other people had to save up for years to see. They actually enjoyed taking in the atmosphere and were glad that we persuaded them to come with us.

We did a show at the hotel on the Friday evening and we left for home on the Saturday. I remember that Barry Sheen, the ex World Champion motorcyclist, was on the flight.

On our return to the UK we added up the amount of flights we had done during the trip and the total came to twenty two! After this we went back on the road and did the odd cruise. Later in the year Derek Franks put a short tour together featuring his acts, Gerry, Tony Christie and Patti. This was in the form of one-nighters, taking in Dartford, Winchester and Hastings, we then flew to Guernsey from Southampton and on to Jersey before finishing in Gloucester.

One trip that summer took us to Germany for a tour of the NAAFI clubs to entertain the troops, taking in Duisburg, Essen, Düsseldorf and Hamlin, where the clock on the Town Hall features the Pied Piper leading away the rats and disappears, then reappears to lead the children away.

One of the sightseeing trips we made was to the Mohnesee Dam where the bouncing bombs of the 'Dam Busters' broke through and there are still two left on show – for the obligatory photos!

Just beyond Hanover was the checkpoint into East Germany, and some of the female border guards even made Bernard Manning look effeminate. Here we took the corridor to Berlin. At this time, if your journey took more than a specified amount of time, you were in trouble and the whole way we were anxious not to break down, you were also in trouble if you arrived too soon – it meant you had been speeding. The route took us past Magdeburg which looked a very foreboding place. Happily, things have changed.

We arrived in Berlin on the Thursday and our show on the Friday, which was to be the first of three, turned out to be our only show there. We were working with a group from Scotland who did a Drifters Tribute Show and we did the first half.

The show took place in a large canteen with a partition down the middle. This was partially opened to about half way down the room and the sound desk was positioned there. In the room were two regiments, one from Scotland in one half and the other from Merseyside in the other half.

During our performance we could feel a rather uneasy atmosphere and when we were finished we went straight back to the 'digs'.

When the Scottish lads arrived back early they told us that a riot had broken out between the two regiments and to get at each other they had to go over the stage, consequently this wrecked all the musical instruments and PA. The roadie/sound engineer received a cut on the nose through being struck by a bottle and had to go to hospital.

The next day we were called back to the barracks for an inquest; the place was like a war zone, blood, broken bottles and glasses all over the floor. It was so bad we had to wipe our feet on the way out and because the equipment was unusable and being unable to replace it, we left immediately for home. Driving through the night to Ostend we caught the five-thirty a.m. ferry and arrived home nine hundred and ninety eight miles later two days early.

Chapter Twenty-Two

Times, They Are A Changing!

All the theatre clubs had good bands and most of them had at least a six-piece, some even had as many as ten pieces. When working theatres we could have as many as sixteen. I always did Patti's arrangements for a line up of four rhythm, two trumpets, one trombone, three saxes, alto tenor and baritone, and string parts which could be played by synthesizer. If we had a conventional big band I used to 'blow them up'.

When Derek Franks started booking for us, some of the first shows we did were with Tony Christie, and this meant using Tony's band, which was very good for Tony and knew his act backwards, but they were not very good sight readers, so these first few gigs were a bit of a struggle to say the least.

Show business was changing. There were not the same amount of venues as before; clubs were closing and there were not as many resident bands as there used to be; a lot of the work was of the one–nighter variety in hotels for private and corporate functions. To get over this lack of backing bands I went in the studio and put down all Patti's arrangements on 'tracks'. I played the piano with Teddy Platt on guitar, Paul Chamberlain on bass and Paul Smith on drums. We now had basic rhythm tracks, and on performances I was able to play the strings or brass parts on synthesiser, along with the tracks.

These days computer programmes are so advanced that we no longer need to go into a studio with a rhythm section. I have now become 'a one man band'. I do every track separately and build up to a full orchestra. This is how the technology of today has put all us trombone players, and the like, out of business! But, I'm afraid that if you can't beat 'em you have to join 'em.

Another thing we had to do was to get a PA system which meant we could work anywhere. Me, who had prided himself on being a first class musician, had now become a bloody roadie! Where once I used to carry just a trombone case and later a briefcase with a baton in it, I was now travelling the country transporting gear. I began to think I was Eddie Stobart! With carrying two synthesisers and stands, six PA speakers and stands, a sound desk, a box of two expensive microphones, a mini disc player, suits, frocks and shoes; we had to change the sleek Toyota Camry for a pantechnicon – sorry, err no, - a Volvo Estate!

So you can see what I mean by "Times; they are a-changing". That was for the ordinary run of the mill type of work, but '89 did prove to be a good year artistically.

Derek put together a show which featured Patti and Tony along with Vince Hill and the *New Squadronaires Orchestra*. It was presented on a nationwide tour by 'Flying Music' and entitled *Swing into Spring.* This was in the early days of the company which has now grown to be one of the largest promoters of touring shows in Great Britain.

I was commissioned by Derek to arrange an opening and closing for the show. For the opening I did a medley of New York songs in which all the artistes were featured.

It started with the orchestra playing a contrapuntal intro of *New York, New York,* from Bernstein's *On the Town* with *Lullaby of Broadway*, and then Patti came on and sang the first sixteen bars of Kander and Ebb's *New York, New York* (that's the Sinatra/ Liza Minnelli one, that everyone sings at chucking out time!) Tony then came on and sang *New York, New York* (this is the "so good they named it twice" one) by Gerard Kenny, and then Vince entered and sang *Lullaby of Broadway*. Patti then went into *Broadway, Broadway*. The three of them then sang *How About You* (that's because it starts with "I like New York in June"). Tony then sang *Manhattan* followed by Patti singing "*NY, NY is a wonderful town"* (writing out New York every time is getting very boring!) after that Vince did *Autumn in NY.* Patti then went into *Give my Regards to Broadway* and after a tap chorus went into *Broadway Melody* with all three of them finishing with *NY, NY* (yes, that one!). It lasted thirteen minutes and I conducted it. I'm proud to say it was one of my best and most original arrangements.

The closing was *Thank You for the Music*, again featuring all three singers and the orchestra. The tour took us all over the UK, including the London Palladium and the BBC recorded the show at the Sunderland Empire which was then broadcast on Radio2, in two one hour parts on two consecutive Saturdays at six o'clock in the evening.

Towards the end of *Swing into Spring* we bought a new Volvo estate and after the tour finished we did every Sunday for eighteen weeks at Butlins, Minehead. It was two hundred and eighty miles door to door so the new car had the best possible 'run-in'. We had that car eleven years, did two hundred and seventy five thousand miles and never used a pint of oil. I think you could say it was WELL run-in!

Come November and we were back on the road with the *Squadronaires* again, this time it was *Swing into Christmas*, with Frankie Vaughan and Stutz Bear Cats. Again it was nationwide, and again we did the Palladium and finished the tour at the Colston Hall in Bristol just before the festive season. Frank and his wife Stella gave us a lovely crystal whisky decanter for a Christmas present, it has pride of place in our cabinet.

The following summer we spent in Ayr at the theatre in Butlins. Patti and Ron Dale, a Scottish comedian, were the resident stars and the rest of the shows were made up of visiting artists among whom were the Grumbleweeds, Alan Stewart and the Chuckle Brothers. I had a five-piece band in the pit. It wasn't one of the best seasons we ever did. The saving grace was that we were paid a lot of money for it, and we have a lovely dining suite, that we bought at the end of the season, which eased the pain and in view of that we call it the 'Butlin Suite'!

Tony Christie, Patti and Vince Hill, *Swing Into Spring*, 1989

Written & Produced by Stuart Atkins

The Magic Of
SAMMY CAHN
FEATURING
Jonathan Lavelle ∗ Patti Gold ∗ Morgan Lee James

A FAX FROM ...
SAMMY CAHN

NY FAX - 212/315-5590   BEV/HILLS FAX - 310/274-4517
TEL - 212/628-8971   TEL - 310/274-7616

Monday
May/3rd
1992.

Dear Stuart, Patti, Terry, Jonathan & Peter -

I have just finished viewing the Video and I am doing what I normally
do when I see something that I think is SPECIAL, I send a FAX!

So here then is a FAX to all of you, - - -

I must say when I sat down and saw the "quality" of video, I didn't think
I would sit through it all, - - -Proof of how great I think it is, I didn't move
from my seat and applauded when it was all over, - - -

As you can imagine "I'VE HEARD THAT SONG BEFORE!" and not just
once but "TIME AFTER TIME!" and each of you did yourselves and my
very very proud, - - -I APPLAUD YOU ALL!!!

Please "cahn-gratulate" the splendid orchestra and all the people BEHIND
the scenes who made it all work, and finally "Sleep with a smile!" you are
each of you very TALENTED!!!

BRAVO! BRAVO!! BRAVO!!!

Sammy Cahn

Sammy was very flattered at
the idea of a show featuring all his
songs, and was very helpful in
putting it together. He did see a
video of the show and was full of
praise for all the performers.

The show tells of his early days
on the Lower East Side of New
York City, to his position as one of
Hollywood's Greatest songwriters.

Among his associates who are mentioned are Jimmy Van
Heusen, Jule Styne, Frank Sinatra, Doris Day, Bing Crosby, and
many, many more of the great stars of the recording and film
industry.

Cahn Comments...

❝ ...proof of how great I thought the video was.
I didn't move from my seat, and applauded when
it was all over... ❞

❝ ...you did yourselves and me very, very proud.
I applaud you all ❞

❝ ...Please "CAHN-GRATULATE" the splendid
orchestra... ❞

❝ ..."SLEEP WITH A SMILE"!! you are each of you very
TALENTED!! ...BRAVO! BRAVO!! BRAVO!! ❞

When once asked, "which comes first, the words or
the music?" Sammy's answer was "The Phone Call"!!!

The Magic Of
SAMMY CAHN

One thing that was palatable was the golf. The local council offered a yearly ticket for £125 which gave you a choice of nine courses to play including Ayr Belle Isle and three municipals at Troon, all top class courses. Even though we only got twenty-two weeks worth it was still excellent value for the money. In July the British Seniors Open took place just down the road at Turnburry and our friend Gwyllam Hardiman, Patti's golf teacher, played in it and we walked around the course with him. We were also able to get close to legends such as Arnold Palmer and Gary Player. In August we drove up to Carnoustie for the day to follow another friend, Martin Jackson, who was playing in the Club Professional's Championship.

Christmas that year wasn't the best.Patti's mother was in hospital having had a bowel operation but happily she came through it. One good thing that did come out of it though was that one afternoon during the holiday Patti had gone to visit her mother, and while she was there I got down to writing something I had been thinking about for quite some time.

The *Swing into Spring* shows we had done with Tony and Vince the year before had been very successful with the two male and one female format and I had an idea to create a show using that, plus a narrator, about my favourite song writer, Sammy Cahn.

This man was one of the most prolific songwriters of all time; he was credited as having put more words into Frank Sinatra's mouth than any other writer and there was a time when he was almost writing exclusively for him. Mr Cahn was nominated no less than twenty-six times for an Oscar and he won four of them. The winning songs were *Three Coins in the Fountain* written with Jule Styne, and *All the Way, High Hopes* and *Call Me Irresponsible* written with James Van Heusen. Only one other person, Johnny Mercer, has won four song writing Oscars. *Love and Marriage* by Cahn and Van Heusen is the only song ever to have won an Emmy which is the TV equivalent of an Oscar.

My thoughts had been that there had been many stage shows written as tributes to people such as the Gershwins, Kerns and Porters, but why must we wait until people are dead before we pay homage to them? So I decided to get on with it, and by the time Pat arrived home I had written the basis of a show.

At the time I subscribed to a bi-monthly American publication called *Sheet Music Magazine* and one of the contributing editors was Sammy Cahn, so I wrote to him, care of the magazine, and told him about the show. What songs I intended to put into medleys, and who would sing what and I also told him who I had worked with over the years and included my CV. I didn't have long to wait for a reply. One Saturday Pat picked me up from the golf club after my morning round and said nothing, but when I got home there waiting for me was an envelope, on it was printed "From the desk of Sammy Cahn" and the address. I was so excited to think that one of my heros had written to me!

He told me that he would be very flattered to have a show written about him and that if I was only half as good as my CV indicated, it was good enough! He told me that if I needed any help he would be delighted to offer any advice I required and that a new album of all his songs had just been published – I already had it!

I sent him a script and piano copies of the medleys I had put together. He was very happy with everything and asked for a recording of the show when finished.

We presented the show, which contained fifty-five of Sammy's songs, at the Leeds Civic Theatre in March '91 featuring Terry Johnson, Jonathan Lavelle, and Patti. The narrator was Peter Levy from BBC Look North TV. Patti and I had known Peter through doing things at Radio Leeds, and he proved to be an inspired choice. Through him a producer at the station organized a link up to Chappell Music in New York, and Sammy and I were recorded being interviewed for the Friday afternoon programme prior to the show on the following Sunday. The interview lasted about an hour, it was the best publicity ever!

I named the show after one of Sammy's songs: *I've Heard that Song Before.*

The show went very well and the audience loved it. We made an audio tape of it and sent it to Sammy who was very impressed, but remarked that he was disappointed it hadn't been a video; not to

Terry, Jonathan and Peter
Leeds Civic Theatre 1991

worry, we did the show at Doncaster Civic Theatre a couple of weeks later and videoed it. I then had it transferred to the American TV system and sent it off. I also sent him the press cuttings of the reviews. I got a reply within two weeks which included a copy of a fax which said:

Dear Stuart,

I have just finished viewing the video and I am doing what I normally do when I see something that I think is SPECIAL, I send a fax!

So here then is a fax to all of you, —

I must say when I sat down and saw the quality of video, I didn't think I would sit through it all,—Proof of how great I think it is, I didn't move from my seat and applauded when it was all over,—

As you can imagine *I'VE HEARD THAT SONG BEFORE!* and not just once but *TIME AFTER TIME*! and each of you did yourselves and me very proud,—I APPLAUD YOU ALL!!!

Please 'cahn-gratulate' the splendid orchestra and all the people BEHIND the scenes who made it all work, and finally "Sleep with a smile" you are each of you very TALENTED!!!

BRAVO! BRAVO!! BRAVO!!!

SAMMY CAHN

I have this fax framed and it has pride of place on my piano! By now, Lee James, who was Derek Franks' brother-in-law and had worked in the office was booking for us and had come up with some nice dates for the show, some in theatres and others in hotels where we presented Dinner/Theatre style shows.

As time went on we were back doing the normal cabaret work as well as the "Sammy" show.

My only regret about the whole Sammy Cahn episode is that I never met him. He invited me to meet him in London in the summer of '93, when he would have been eighty years old, but unfortunately he died in the January of that year. A shame, but it wasn't to be.

Chapter Twenty-Three

I Am Sailing, I Am Sailing - -

In autumn '92 we did a cruise on the *Black Prince* which sailed from Tilbury. As we were checking in a young man was doing so at the same time and introduced himself. I did the same and Patti said: "Hello, I'm Patti Gold", and his reply was: "Of course you are", which was rather funny, and we laughed about it. He said: "I recognised you from the telly"! The young man's name was Morgan Lee James and he was, like us, one of the guest acts for this cruise.

This was the first cruise we had done for Fred Olsen Line. It was a small ship which in an earlier life had been a car ferry, however it was very pleasant. The band wasn't great. They were Filipinos and weren't very good readers, but we managed to get through. Over the two weeks we became very good friends with Morgan and on one of the cabaret spots he joined Patti and me on stage to sing a medley of songs that I had done for the Sammy Cahn show, it went very well.

Another cruise we did for Olsen was to the Canaries calling at most of the islands. One memory that stands out is after leaving

La Gomera, on which I believe the Olsen Company have a huge banana plantation, on a Sunday morning and the church service had just finished, we hit a rogue wave and the upright piano, which was suspended to the wall on heavy metal hooks, flew up into the air and fell to the floor. Why it is memorable is because the pianist who had played for the service had just put down the piano lid and was literally walking away when this happened. When he turned and saw the piano he went ashen white and raised his eyes heavenward, crossed himself, and said: "Thank you"!

Back home we had done a couple of dates with the Sammy show and Terry Johnson had been very forgetful and had slipped up a couple of times. To be fair to Terry he was a good stylish singer in the Sinatra mould but he had never been a "pro" and his stagecraft was minimal. Because we were getting more bookings for the show I decided that I needed to replace Terry and I offered the gig to Morgan. He was very happy to accept, so, after some hard rehearsals, with Jonathan and Patti, we had a stronger team.

We did the show in York, Manchester, Tadcaster, Wakefield (with a ten piece band), Burnley, Hull and Chesterfield. When we did the show in Warrington I didn't have a narrator so my agent friend Don Jones did it for us. I wonder if he paid himself any commission!

For the Chesterfield show, Morgan arranged for David Llewellyn to come along and see it. David was the booking manager for P&O Cruises and Morgan had done a few cruises for them. Thankfully, he liked what he saw and immediately booked us to do a two week cruise to Aqaba in Jordan on *MV Sea Princess*. We went via the Mediterranean, calling at various ports on the way, and the Suez Canal. Morgan and Patti did cabaret spots and then we did the first half of the Sammy show one evening and followed it with the second half the next. It was a great success and was the start of what was to become the main source of our work in the nineties.

When we arrived back home David Llewellyn rang and told us he had had good reports about us all and booked us to do the first leg from Southampton to San Francisco on *MV Canberra* of the '93 World Cruise. Not a bad result.

We boarded the ship at lunchtime on the 6th January to be greeted by the Cruise Director Ian Frazer and were shown to our quarters on 'G' Deck which was called 'Equity Court' for obvious reasons. We shared the accommodation with all the other 'turns', Morgan, comedian Tommy Sutton and the resident theatre company.

Hughie Taylor was Cruise Director on *Sea Princess* and was very happy for us to do our Sammy Cahn show in two parts as booked by David Llewellyn but not Mr Frazer. He didn't want it over two nights and he made it obvious that he was in charge and not some administrator from Head Office. So I condensed the two acts into one and made a few cuts to the script and presented the show in one performance. We got the impression that Mr Frazer didn't care much for us, and even more so after the show went well, especially as the Americans were very complimentary.

From Southampton we sailed to Madeira which took us five days, we had very calm seas then to St. Kits and after that we went to Caracas in Venezuela and then on to Cristobel at the start of what was to be the highlight of the trip, the day we went through the Panama Canal.

On the morning of the transfer we awoke to find we were at

anchor awaiting our turn to proceed and as we looked towards the entrance I could see a group of trees and above them I could see a ship! This looked so surreal but then it dawned on me that the ship was in the first lock. When it was our turn to go through the locks it was very interesting to note that on each side of the ship the gap to the lock sides was only a matter of inches. The new *QMII* cannot go through the Panama because she is too wide!

At the Caribbean side of the canal we went up three locks and on the Pacific side we went down two. I can't explain how but I do believe that the Pacific Ocean is higher than the Atlantic. After the first locks the canal opens out into a large lake with the channel marked out by buoys, then as it gets nearer to the other end it narrows down to a gorge cut out of rock. Throughout the day we saw beautiful birds, parrots, parakeets, canaries of all different colours and pelicans.

We arrived at Panama City in the evening and tied up for a couple of hours. In the sheds along the quayside the local traders were selling their wares to the tourists. It had been a great day!

The Panama is different to the Suez in as much as it is wide enough for ships to pass each other, whereas in the Suez a number of ships head south in convoy to a great lake half way down at Ismailiya, then the convoy waiting in the lake heads north and the southern convoy waits for the ships in the bottom part of the canal to arrive in the lake then the convoy heading south continues through to the Red Sea. Each convoy has about a four-hour wait in the lake at Ismailiya.

From Panama City we continued our journey, next stop Acapulco. It certainly is a place to write a song about. We anchored in the bay and went ashore by tender, then we took a taxi to the famous rocks where the locals dive into the sea from a great height for coins. From there we went to a lovely beach for a couple of hours, stopping off along the way at a place with a huge cross which we had seen from the ship whilst at anchor. It was an International Peace Garden and it was so quiet you could hear the silence!

On leaving Acapulco we sailed up the west coast of America and with the use of binoculars we could see the naval dockyards as we passed San Diego, then on past Catalina Island, where the legendary Errol Flynn and stars of that era used to spend their weekends yachting – plus whatever else might take their fancy!

Three days later we arrived in San Francisco, unfortunately we didn't see much of it as we were transferred to the plane for the flight home at lunch-time, but we rectified that on our next visit.

Waikiki Beach

We hadn't been home very long before we got a call from Mr Llewellyn asking us to fly to Sydney in a week's time to pick up *Sea Princess*, which was circumnavigating the world the opposite way to *Canberra*.

We flew out to Sydney arriving at midnight. Some of the crew who were taking over from their colleagues who were going on leave were also on the flight and we all stayed the night at the very nice Lawson Hotel. We were picked up next morning and transferred to the ship.

Morgan was also on this trip with us and in the afternoon we had a message to go to see David Llewellyn who had boarded the same day, unbeknown to us. After the pleasantries and the offer of a drink, David said: "What happened on *Canberra*? You didn't do very well." After a pause of amazement Patti and I went berserk which completely threw him. We pointed out that both Patti's and Morgan's cabaret spots, as well as the Sammy Cahn show, all had standing ovations. I realised at that moment that cruise directors want visiting artists to be good - BUT NOT TOO GOOD! I said this to David and asked him to make up his own mind after he had seen Patti's next cabaret show. It went great. Another 'stander'!

He left the ship in Fiji to fly back to the UK and said he would be in touch, but we were all disappointed with Ian Frazer's report and weren't sure what to expect. However we just had to get on with things.

After Fiji we called in Honolulu and while there we went to Waikiki beach and Pearl Harbour and it was very interesting to see the Arizona Memorial.

We left the ship at Long Beach. This time I had booked a night in a hotel before we left home so we were able to do some sight seeing. We went up to Hollywood and while we were there an earthquake took place which was quite high on the Richter Scale which made all the news media worldwide, everyone was talking about it and guess what – we never felt a thing!

While there we went to look at The Walk of Stars and naturally we looked for, and found, Sammy's star. We also found Sinatra's star as well as Louis Armstrong's, who had said to Patti when at Batley, "Nice woiking wit you". This from a superstar to a sixteen year old!

Next day we flew from LA up to San Francisco for four days before flying home. When we checked into the hotel where we were staying a

Hollywood!

fax was waiting for us from David Llewellyn booking us for cruises for the whole of May, June, and July. Up yours Mr Frazer!

San Francisco was all we had been led to believe it to be. We stayed in a Travel Lodge Hotel opposite Tower Records, which had the most comprehensive range of music I have ever seen, just off Ghirardelli Square. I was fascinated by all the art and photo galleries around this area. Some of these places exhibited limited edition prints of clowns which turned out to have been painted by Red Skelton, who apparently specialised in painting clowns. Close by is the cable car terminus from where the service starts and goes all the way to Union Square. The Ghirardelli family were chocolate makers, and the main building, which dominates the area and carries the huge neon Ghirardelli sign, was the old factory.

The Golden Gate Bridge, Pier 39, Fisherman's Wharf, the sea lions in the Wharf, Alcatraz, Lombard Street, Nob Hill; these are all the things about San Francisco which makes everyone want to leave their heart there and return. I've certainly left my heart there and, along with Sydney, it shares the top position in the league table of favourite places I've ever been to. Happily I've returned to them both many times since.

Chapter Twenty-Four

Celebrity Golf

The cruise to Aqaba in November '92 was the start of an association with P&O cruises which lasted until '98. After those world cruises in '93 the ones in the summer of that year started at Southampton and went to places as far afield as St Petersburg, Yalta on the Black Sea in the East, to the Canary Isles in the South, the North Cape in the Arctic Circle and all places in between.

From the beginning of October to early December we cruised out of Venice every two weeks with a two-day turn around. We did this for about four successive years. We got to know the place very well and loved every minute of it. Some of the churches had wonderful paintings by Canaletto and Titian in them. All the cruises called in at various Greek Islands and usually paid a visit to Istanbul. This is another fascinating place. The Grand Bazaar is the largest I have ever seen, and you can buy anything from a safety pin to a camel. The ships tie up on the Golden Horn at the mouth of the Bosporus and from there you can look across and see the hospital where Florence Nightingale attended the

179

wounded of the Crimean War. Other sights to see included the Topkapi Palace and the Blue Mosque.

On our visits home we did a few gigs of the Sammy Cahn show with Morgan, Jonathan and Peter. I also did a version for the ships which Patti and I did as a 'two hander'.

In early '94 we flew to Singapore to pick up *Victoria* – this was the *Sea Princess* as was, but after transfer from Princess Cruises to P&O, the name was changed to something more British. From there we went to Vietnam, and then sailed into Hong Kong just before midnight on Chinese New Year's Eve. There was a great atmosphere in the place. Of course we had to go to Stanley Market again to restock the sequined dresses! When we boarded the Star Ferry to go across to the Island the first thing we saw – as if to make us feel at home – was an advert for Harry Ramsden's Hong Kong fish and chip shop which had opened since we were there before.

Our next stop was Kota Kinabalu on the island of Borneo. On arrival we went to a resort hotel for the day and along with Morgan and a few other people from the ship we settled down to a day around the pool. Next to us was a young man who was obviously English and was reading some papers which I happened to get a glance of. I noticed that they were headed Coutts & Co and thought that he was a yuppie from the Stock Exchange on holiday with his attractive blonde wife. It wasn't until two weeks later when we were in the lounge of Singapore Airport on the way back home, having stopped for refuelling, that I realised who our sunlounger neighbour had been. It was Nick Leeson, and the TV was showing pictures of his arrest in Frankfurt. When we arrived home I saw photos of him and his wife in all the Sunday papers and this confirmed everything to me.

From KK we called in at Darwin in the Northern Territories of Australia. It was a Saturday and was probably the only non event of the cruise. What a boring place it turned out to be, there was hardly anyone around. I think the highlight of the day was watching the traffic lights change!

The next stop was totally different. Hamilton Island on the Great Barrier Reef; this was beautiful. This is one of a group of islands known as the Whit Sundays. The water was crystal clear and we could see all the species of fish swimming in shoals showing off their beautiful colours. The island itself was lovely with beautiful beaches, palm trees, lovely houses, a few first class hotels, and a picturesque little church where a wedding was taking place.

Two days later we were going through the North and South Heads, the entrance to Sydney Harbour. It was six-thirty in the morning and every one was up to catch a first glimpse of the 'Coat Hanger', as the famous bridge is known locally. As we drew nearer we could just see the top of the bridge and then as we went around another corner we saw a bit more of it and then when there were no more corners to go around. The whole of the harbour opened up before us and there it was, the bridge, the Opera House, the Centre Point Tower and all the skyline of downtown Sydney. We left the ship and had a few days in Sydney with Paul Eddison, a singer who had been working on the cruise with us, before returning home.

We weren't home long before we were flying to San Fran to do the last leg of the *Canberra* World Cruise. We went three days early and had a break before the ship came in. Among our fellow entertainers were Bobby Knutt, the comedian, with his wife Donna (Donna Hartley as was - the runner) and Gerard Kenny, the American singer/songwriter; his most famous songs being the *Minder* theme which was sung by Dennis Waterman and *I Made it Through the Rain* recorded by Barry Manilow. Don Jones was, and still is, Gerard's manager and was booking for Patti and me at this time.

The cruise back to Southampton was a reversal of the first time we had sailed on *Canberra* the year before. Acapulco being the first stop, and going the opposite way through the Panama. Oh, by the way, I got myself a Big Bertha driver from a golf shop on this trip. I was the first person at my club to have one - they were five hundred quid in England then but I paid two hundred and seventy dollars for it in the States.

The trouble with doing the last leg of a World Cruise is that the inmates (passengers) are stir crazy by this time and are grumpy and short tempered, so it takes the acts a lot of effort and patience to entertain them, but we all did our best and finished the cruise in style.

Back on dry land we did the usual cabaret gigs but work wasn't as plentiful as before. One thing that contributed to this was that people knew we were doing a lot of cruising now and as a consequence the phone stopped ringing. In the summer we did eight weeks in Scarborough with the *Black and White Minstrels* at the Opera House produced by John Redgrave who, when working for him in Torbay in '77 I thought was ok, but he turned out to be a con artist, because throughout the run we had nothing but trouble with money, delays in payment, bouncing cheques, excuses and rows. We did eventually get everything we were entitled to but it was a very unhappy season.

In between the cruises and the summer season Don Jones came up with a few corporate functions, some of them were with a quartet I put together to accompany Gerard Kenny on his gigs.

One gig that Patti and I did was at the Belfry Hotel in Warwickshire. The Black Abbots were on the bill with us, and knowing that Pat had started playing golf asked if we would be interested in playing on the Celebrity Golf Tour. We said we would and they told the person who ran the organisation, Paul Gaskell, and he rang us offering some dates, the first of which was a tournament at Matfen Hall near Newcastle.

The first time we met Paul we knew that this was someone we could get along with. He made us feel very welcome and he treated us as part of the team from the off. The tour is made up of sportsmen and women, actors and entertainers, some we knew, and others we were to get to know and become good friends with. Among the sports personalities were footballers such as Phil Neal, Tony Curry, Alan Ball, Roger Hunt, David Fairclough, Graham Sharp, Howard Kendall, Roy Evans, Peter Nicholson, Willie Morgan, Ian St. John, Trevor Cherry and my hero from his Huddersfield Town days, Frank Worthington. Frank Myler, Steve Hampson, and Reg Bowden from Rugby League and cricketers Brian Close, Farouk Engineer, Graham Roope, David Hughes and Denis Amiss were all regulars, as were boxer Jackie Turpin and wrestler Al Markett.

The show business lot included Trevor Bannister, Johnny Briggs, Garfield Morgan, Shaun Tudor Owen, Tim Healey, Tony Barton, Kevin Whatley, Duncan Preston and John Bowe, all actors. Then came the 'turns'. Stan Boardman, his son Paul, who is now an anchor man on Sky Sports News, Johnny More, Max Peters, Dickey Day, Brendan Healey, Mickey Gunn, Roger De Corsey, Mick Miller, Stan Stennett and Sir Norman Wisdom were some of the comedians. I would often accompany Sir Norman when he sang *Don't Laugh at Me* on the shows. I was probably the only one old enough to remember it! The singers included Con Clusky, Danny Roman, Tony Christie, Pat O Hare, Dean Andrews, Bryan Johnson of AC/DC, Billy Mitchell of Lindisfarne and Jeff Hill of the Houghton Weavers, singer/guitarist John Miles and pianist Rick Wakeman. These are just some of the regular players, but there are many other household names who do the odd tournament, depending on commitments.

Paul was a great organizer and the days went like clockwork. We would be booked in to a first class hotel the evening before the tournament and sometimes there would be a reception at the golf club we were to play. The day of the tournament would start with sandwiches and coffee on arrival, each team would be allocated a 'celeb' and a 'shotgun start' would take place at around lunchtime. In the evening there would be a banquet where Paul would introduce all the celebrities between the first course, then there would be stand up bingo between the next, and then some of the singers would sing a couple of numbers. At the end of the meal the prizegiving would take place followed by a charity auction, after which some of the entertainers would put on a show which would last about an hour and a half, but if we couldn't find a cupboard to lock Stan Boardman in it would be three or four hours long!

One memorable Tour event took place at my own club, Howley Hall, near Leeds. Patti and I took our friend Steve Bestwick, who happened to be the financial director of the club, to one of the meetings at Carden Park and he thought it would be a good idea to have a Celebrity Am tournament at Howley, after seeing how Paul ran these golf days. So a committee was formed and it was decided to have a Festival week which comprised of various competitions and social events.

The Festival week started with Ladies Day on the Saturday followed by a mixed competition on the Sunday. On the Monday we had a line dancing evening which was run by Donna Hartley MBE, the former champion athlete. Tuesday we had an open four ball. Wednesday was party night; this was when all the celebs turned up on the evening before the main event on the Thursday and some of the entertainers did a few turns for the members. This also allowed the members to mix with the stars, have a chat and get autographs and photos with their favourites such as Sir Norman Wisdom, Tony Curry, Eddie 'the Eagle' Edwards, Frank Worthington, Trevor Bannister et al.

The Celeb/Am day went excellently with Patti's team of Alison Mowat, Jean Grimbleby, and Penny Bestwick winning first prize of the competition and I won the Celebrity prize. Taking part in the cabaret in the evening was Johnny More, whose impressions are terrific, Norman Collier, who had every one in stitches – as usual! Mickey Gunn was funny, and John Miles included in his spot - especially for Patti – his great hit *Music Was My First Love.* A great day was had by all. On Friday we had a seniors open and we finished off the week with a men's competition on the Saturday for the Centenary Vase and in the evening we had a casino night. It was a great week at the end of which we were able to present money to a few charities and the main donation of five thousand pounds went to ARC, the arthritis charity, which was suggested by Patti in view of the help she has had in her battle with the disease. Altogether it was a successful week which we repeated for the next few years.

Sadly Paul died in early 2004 at the age of 54 and had only been married to Catherine for about six months. They had both been married before and the wedding took place at Carden Park after the last Celeb Golf event of the 2003 season with most of us who played on the tour present. Howard Kendal was his best man. Catherine took over the running of the tour initially but I don't think her heart was in it so Paul's friend Alan Clark took on the task. Although things are done exactly as before and Alan books the same players, but with Paul not being there, there is a void, and although it is no one's fault, things are not the same because Paul Gaskell *was* The Celebrity Golf Tour.

Prior to playing on the Celebrity Tour we had taken part in a few charity golf events run by other people, one of whom was John Farrar, who organized, among others, the Geoffrey Boycott Classic which took place at the Welcombe Hotel in Stratford-on-Avon every year, and I used to provide the band, which one year included Jerry Freeman, Shirley Bassey's drummer. Sadly, John who besides organizing golf events used to run sportsmen's benefit funds, is no longer with us.

Les Simpson was another organizer of golf events we played for, and we have remained friends ever since.

A group called LEGS - an anachronism of the Lancashire Entertainers Golf Society - used to invite us to some of their charity meetings also. I remember one time we were playing at a course in Ingle near Preston, which was organized by Sam Homer – a

186

singer – for LEGS. I had received a call from Sam asking if I could bring any other 'celebs' I knew to make up the field and I suggested our friends Alison and Ian Mowat. They had taken part in other celebrity events because Alison had been an international swimmer for England and played ladies golf for Yorkshire, and her husband Ian was an Irish international discus and shot put champion who also played Rugby Union for Morley and Yorkshire. Unfortunately it turned out that Alison and Ian could not make it that day due to other commitments, but we had a solution. These two people happen to be the proud parents of two of the most gorgeous girls you could ever set eyes upon. Angela is tall and statuesque with legs up to her armpits, and looks to die for, and Rebecca, also tall and equally beautiful with long blonde hair and, like her mother, played golf for Yorkshire Ladies. So Patti and I took Rebecca, who calls us Auntie Patti and Uncle Stuart, with us. I tell you our stock went up in leaps and bounds that day! We

were registering at the desk and Sam looked up and did a double take and mouthed the words at me "——— 'ell"! After being introduced to 'our niece' he said, "I'll introduce you to your team". He went over to three big lads, rugby players, and

Tom O'Conner
Riviera Centre Torquay 1995

pointing over to Rebecca, said: "That is your celebrity, lads", at which point all three of them, just as Sam had, exclaimed, "——— 'ell"! Rebecca, wearing a mini skirt, and with her long blonde hair and her tanned legs was making quite an impression on everyone around, but that wasn't all. When she and her team went to the first tee everyone in the club house went to the windows to watch and after the three lads had teed off with decent shots Rebecca took her place on the ladies tee, which was only about ten yards in front of the men's, and launched a drive just like an exocet missile which split the fairway and landed only about fifty yards from the green, and the reaction from all the fellows watching from the club house was – yes, just as before: "———- 'ell!" Rebecca, now Mrs Ed Palmer, is the Vice Consul for Trade and Investment at the British Consulate in New York, and I am sure that had she not opted for commerce she would have made it on the ladies pro golf tour.

In early '95 we did a couple of months in the Caribbean on *Victoria*. All the cruises started from San Juan in Puerto Rico, and did various permutations of itineraries for visiting the different islands. During this period I had a permanent suntan. I think my favourite island was St. Lucia but they all had their good points. I enjoyed Antigua, Barbados, and Stingray City in Grand Cayman, this is a sand bank about three miles off the coast where you can swim with these marvellous creatures. The boatmen who take you out throw raw meat for them and they brush against you while swimming around. I also liked the Dutch Antilles; Aruba and Bonaire in particular.

In the summer we did six weeks at the Riviera Centre in Torquay with Tom O'Connor and the Nolan Sisters. Cannon and Ball were supposed to do this season, but according to Bobby Ball he had a vision telling him that they should go to America, so they pulled out of the contract, leaving Don to fix a show at short notice. I suppose Tom O'Connor and ourselves should be grateful for the divine intervention of the Great Impresario in the sky! Tom, Patti and I played quite a bit of golf together during the six weeks, and one of the courses we played was Churston, where I had first started to play in the summer of '77 with the Bachelors.

Cruising and Celebrity Tour Golf took up most of '96. One of the cruises took us to the Baltic. We sailed via the Kiel Canal which is in the North West corner of Germany near the boarder with Denmark. The canal goes through lovely flat countryside and to see a big ship in the middle of fields and passing under autobahn bridges is quite surreal. After Kiel our first call was in Stockholm, then on to Helsinki and St. Petersburg. A lot of the buildings and roads in St. Petersburg were in a bad state of repair but a lot of work was taking place bringing the city back to its pre-Communist state. The Tsar's Winter Palace and the Hermitage Museum, with the pastel painted cream and green walls with gold leaf trim were spectacular. On the way back we called at Gdansk in Poland and saw the famous shipyard where the Solidarity Union started, and our last call was Copenhagen. A big band was playing on the bandstand in Tivoli Gardens and it was very good indeed, playing the music of Kenton, Basie and Miller and they had a very good girl singer with them.

Come Christmas we did a cruise to the Canaries on *Canberra.* This was the first time we had been away at Christmas, but it turned out to be very enjoyable. As you would expect the food was superb and the highlight of the trip was New Year's Eve. In Madeira on New Year's Eve, the most fantastic firework display takes place, and there are usually at least a dozen cruise ships at anchor in the Bay of Funchal. The fireworks start at one side of the town and go all around the bay to the other side and from the town itself up into the mountains. Apart from the Sydney Millennium display on TV it is the most spectacular I have ever seen.

In February '97 we flew to San Francisco again and had four days holiday before joining *Oriana* for the San Fran/Sydney leg of the world cruise. On joining the ship, Hughie Taylor, the cruise director, asked me if I would do some golf coaching in the nets as he didn't have a golf coach on board. I said I would, and although I wasn't a qualified coach I had helped people with their game before, so I was quite happy to do two hours every morning while the ship was at sea. I enjoyed the experience and when some of my pupils came back on board after playing in Hawaii they were very complimentary and said that was the best they had ever played.

After Hawaii we called in Tahiti. Where the ship docked we could see a small island with a mountain, this was the location used for the island of Bali Ha'i in the film *South Pacific*. We then went on to Auckland before our disembarkation in Sydney. Because I had done the golf coaching for him Hughie Taylor paid my bar bill!

We stayed in Sydney for five days to await the arrival of *Canberra*, on which we were booked back to San Francisco, this time with the penultimate call in Vancouver.

Our stay in Sydney was wonderful as usual, we stayed at the Lawson Hotel near Darling Harbour and had great days out in the various parts of the city. Manley beach, Mona Vale and Palm Beach – this is where they film *Home and Away,* and you know what? Patti and I never miss an episode; how sad is that!? Joking apart – it is a beautiful place and it brings back happy memories.

One day we went up Centre Point Tower where you have a

three hundred and sixty degree view of the area. In one direction you can see as far as the Blue Mountains. The next day we went up there to Katoomba, the capital of the Blue Mountains National Park. The reason for the name is because there is always a blue haze in the air and this comes from the sap of all the eucalyptus trees. On the outskirts of Katoomba are three tall outcrops of rock called the Three Sisters. Legend has it that they were turned to stone by their father because he didn't approve of their respective lovers.

After five days *Canberra* arrived on what was her last visit to Sydney, this was her last world cruise and she was being retired after this. She had had a long association with Australia. A lot of the 'ten pound' emigrants had sailed on her and the England Cricket Test teams always used her before flying became the way of things.

Canberra 1997
Final World Voyage

As we boarded there were hundreds of people crowding around the quayside and tons of streamers being thrown both from and to the ship. We pulled away and it was very emotional as we left the Harbour Bridge behind us and said goodbye to the Opera House on our starboard side. We were accompanied by a flotilla of boats all the way to the Sydney Heads harbour entrance passing Rose Bay, Watson's Bay, Mosman, and Manley.

Overhead three TV news helicopters recorded the whole scene.

After the excitement of our departure we did our usual entertaining and we were delighted to meet Victor Borge who was going home on the ship after a tour of Australia – would you believe, he was ninety-three at this time? And Patrick Lichfield, who was one of the lecturers.

Our first stop was Western Samoa and then Honolulu and Maui. After that we went to Vancouver, which is a lovely place, and the Canadian people were so friendly. When we arrived in San Fran we flew straight home as we had been away for two months and, as always, we couldn't wait to have fish and chips, and jam and bread after all that rich food we had had to put up with!

On our way home from Heathrow we called in for a celebrity golf day at Stoke Poges. The first person to greet us in the clubhouse was Frankie Vaughan, who was having tea with Howard Keel, and he invited us to join them. Howard turned out to be just as charming a person as Frank and I played with him in a four ball along with Johnny Mathis and John Miles of *Music was my First Love* fame, a few years later at Carden Park, which is the headquarters of the Celebrity Golf Tour.

The Celebrity Golf Tour enabled me to play a lot of first class golf courses, such as the Forrest of Arden, St Pierre, Motram Hall, Royal Birkdale and Hoylake.

Celeb Golf Tour at Howley Hall

Me and Willie Morgan

Chapter Twenty-Five

The End Of The Voyage

In spring we flew back to the Caribbean and did more cruising on *Victoria.* I enjoyed the cruising in the Caribbean, it was always good weather and the islands were beautiful. The first cruise of this contract took us to Tampa where we met up with our friends Derek and Carol Harper who had a home in Sarasota; I've mentioned Derek before, he played trumpet for me in the big band and he used to augment at Batley. They had the house for a few years and used to spend the winters there. Sadly, Derek died a few years ago, he was a very good friend and Patti and I miss him greatly. Patti gave the eulogy at his funeral starting with the words; "So who's going to make us laugh now"? He was just a fun kind of guy and his musician friends had a 'blow' at his wake. He would have loved it!

After Tampa we went to Key West which was very nice. I remember the bar where Ernest Hemmingway used to drink, and we had the best lobster meal ever in a dockside restaurant that was nothing more than a wooden shack.

On the last cruise of this contract Cannon and Ball came on

board to work and they brought their families with them. It turned out that I knew Tom's wife, Hazel, she was one of the Tiller Girls in the '76 summer season Bachelors Show I had conducted at the Bournemouth Pavilion.

On every cruise, on the last Thursday, they have what is called Tropicana Night. This is very casual where everyone dresses in tropical type clothing and the show takes place around the swimming pool. This particular show started with the resident theatre company opening with a *South Pacific* medley which finished with the song *There is Nothing Like a Dame*, at the end of which one of the 'sailors' in the routine is pushed into the pool. After this Hughie Taylor the Cruise Director came on, did a five minute warm up, and then introduced Patti. I started the band in what is called a round and round ad lib intro – that's a certain number of bars being repeated until the artiste gets to the microphone.

As Patti got to the mike she slipped and fell on her back. I kept the intro going and the DJ Steve West, along with Hughie Taylor, dashed on to help her to her feet. She completed the act but was in a lot of pain. Bobby Ball was watching from the back of the audience and thought "what a great opening". At that point he thought it was deliberate. What happened was the theatre company changed every three months and this was the first cruise of a new company.

The boy who was dumped in the water at the end of the opening should have been told to exit the pool, go behind the people sitting alongside and back to the dressing area up the side steps, unfortunately he came out of the pool, went straight across the stage, up the steps which led from the stage, and as he did so he left a trail of water, consequently, when Patti was introduced she entered the stage down the steps and slipped on the wet deck landing on her back.

After a few years of fighting, and a court case, she eventually received substantial damages. This took place in 2003. Bobby Ball said he would be a witness should it come to court, but when the time came, he didn't want to know. I understand he is a Born Again Christian; the phrase "and some passed by on the other side" from the parable of The Good Samaritan springs to mind!

Vince Hill's wife Anne was a witness. She couldn't be there because they were working in America but she sent a very detailed letter, and Steve West came all the way from Cornwall. The trial was at York Crown Court and Hughie Taylor was the main witness for P&O. In the anti room to the court the atmosphere was a little strained with Hughie being there, but on reflection I don't hold anything against him, because after all he was representing P&O and they did pay his wages. We won anyway!

The last cruise we did for P&O was Christmas '97 in the Caribbean. I didn't like it! On Christmas Eve we were in beautiful Aruba, Christmas day at sea, and Boxing Day was spent on a beautiful beach in Tobago, it was awful. You're probably thinking 'ungrateful so and so' I'm sorry, but I like my Christmases with snow!

The penultimate day of the cruise we were at anchor off Granada and the *Oriana* was also there. Some of the band had been over to the *Oriana* and had had quite a heavy drinking session with their musicians. Back on board *Victoria* at the five o'clock band call, the trumpet player was worse for wear. I was rehearsing Patti's music and when we came to the arrangement I had done of the Peggy Lee version of *The Folks Who Live on the Hill,* I blew my top. The intro to the song starts with a very plaintive trumpet taking the lead, and this is probably one of the most famous easy listening records ever made, so it is very well known. The trumpet player was so drunk that he couldn't play it. I balled him out; I shouted at the bandleader for allowing this to happen, and I went mad with the stage manager. As I said, it was our last cruise!

The next morning before we left, Albert, the trumpet player, came not to apologise, but to carry on the row. We nearly got to blows; it's a pity really, because he is a good player. But not that day!

We met a lot of very nice people throughout our cruising period, some we had known before, but through spending more time in a confined space with people you get to know them better.

Ray Allen and his wife Jane became good friends, Bobby Knutt and Donna, Tom Sutton and his wife, singer Joanne Shields, Vince and Anne Hill and Gerard Kenny. Some of the other people who were interesting to meet were Victor Borge and Patrick Lichfield who I told you about on the last *Canberra* cruise and Richard Baker, the former BBC newsreader.

Richard used to present three classical music cruises a year on P&O ships, which were organised by a very nice lady called Stephanie Williams, and we were fortunate to be on some of them. Tasmin Little, the international violinist, and concert pianists Martin Ruscoe and Peter Donahoe were on one of them, Susan Drake, a very fine harpist was on another and singers Marilyn Hill-Smith, Janine Roebuck and Ian Caddy were on two that we did.

One classical cruise that I enjoyed was when Richard asked all the light entertainment artistes, along with the classical people to take part in a 'Last Night at the Proms' type finale. The Schidlov String Quartet was on this cruise and I arranged *The Way you Look Tonight* for them, and they accompanied Patti on *Somewhere over the Rainbow.* At Richard's request I arranged *Rule Britannia* and *Land of Hope and Glory* for the whole company, using the resident band augmented by the string quartet, the harpist, piano duettists Anthony Goldstone and Caroline Clemmow and all the singers. Janine started it all off in costume dressed as Britannia. All that was missing was the grand organ!

All the cruises always had a classical pianist on them. I got to know and became friends with many of them, including: Alan Schiller, Vincent Billington, Veronica McSweeney and Elizabeth Hays.

So our association with P&O came to an end and we now had to start looking around for other work. The phone had stopped ringing and you start to panic a little. I rang a few agents and slowly we started to get work again and later in the year we did three cruises for Saga including the '98 Christmas cruise. Again this was to the Canaries, but the fireworks on New Year's Eve didn't last as long as the first time we saw them, so we felt a bit cheated.

A few weeks after the cruise Patti rang Saga enquiring about other cruises and she spoke to the new man in charge who said she hadn't made the ratings. At the end of all cruises the passengers are asked to assess the standards of all the services they are presented with; food, cabins, meals, tours, entertainment etc., and make any comments they may have. This took her somewhat by surprise because after every show she had a standing ovation. He had seen the ratings and had the cruise director's report which said, "- and some people stood up". Patti pointed out that everyone who was able did stand up, all the others were in wheel chairs! Prat! So that was the end of our cruising!

It didn't matter, because as the saying goes; "when one door closes, another one bangs in your face" – no, not really – another one happened to open. I had a call from Lee James asking me if I could put a band together to tour with someone he had found. This young man had been doing a Sinatra tribute show with backing tracks, but Lee thought he would give it a go in the theatres with a big band. I had a meeting with Lee and his protégé, James Chadwick, who sang a couple of songs for me, and yes, he did sound like 'The Governor'.

As I talked to him it was obvious that James didn't have a lot of stage experience so Patti and I had a few meetings with him and gave him tips and we wrote a script for him and made out a balanced programme. I arranged an introduction of *My Way* and *New York* with the announcement over a timpani roll, then straight into *Come Fly with Me.* This worked very well, even though he did lack stagecraft the audience seemed to like him, and we went on a nationwide tour from as far afield as Billingham in the north to Worthing in the south. The show was called *Sinatra: All the Way* with the band playing the first half and James doing the second.

One thing I remember and smile about was that after *Come Fly with Me* the script we had written for him went on to tell how the next number – *I've Got the World on a String* – was on the 'A' side of Sinatra's first recording for Capitol Records and that the session should have been arranged and conducted by Billy May; this didn't happen because Billy May was on tour with his band, so Nelson Riddle was brought in for the session and even though the 'B' side, *South of the Border* says "arranged by Billy May" – it was in fact done by Nelson Riddle in the style of Billy May.

The reason I smile is because James, with his lack of stage craft, would relate this story to the audience in his Sheffield accent which went something like; "This next song wor-arranged by Nelson Riddle burr it shudda bin dun by Billy May, but Billy wo ron tour at 'time wi'' 'is band, so it were dun by Nelson, in Billy's styal". Every time we came to this part of the show I would be facing the band with my toes curling and looking at Mike Cox, with each of us trying not to laugh! James was a nice guy and he sang well but I'm afraid he lacked a little something in the presentation department.

I had some great players on this tour. Tom Steer was the pianist with Dave Lynaine on bass, Teddy Platt, guitar and Ronnie Bottomley or John Gilbert on drums. Dale Gibson was lead trumpet, big Derek Southcott was on lead trombone and Bill Charleson, Steve DeVine, Norman Brown, Mike Cox and Mike Hale were in the sax section; it was a super band and all those Nelson Riddle, Billy May and Don Costa arrangements sounded terrific.

Chapter Twenty-Six

Full Circle

The first chapter in this book recalls the time I spent in York during my National Service and how we, the squaddies, used to meet in Betty's Bar at the start of a night out, well, I am now, some fifty years later, the regular Wednesday evening pianist at Betty's Tea Rooms in York, which means the wheel has turned full circle. The bar was below ground floor in those days but today the shop and tearooms take up the ground and below floors. They have a café pianist from 6pm to 9pm every evening and 10am to 1pm on Sunday morning.

I became associated with Betty's through two friends of mine, Beryl and Peter Jackson, who are regular customers at the Harrogate branch. One day they were talking to the pianist there and happened to say they had a friend who was a musician. The pianist was Derry Jones who is also the fixer for Bettys' pianists. It so happened that Derry had written a song which I recorded with Cool Breeze in the 70's, but he didn't know I was available for gigs. Like everyone else he thought I would be constantly on the road; but when he knew I wasn't, he rang and offered me some work. It started out as dep jobs but then regular Wednesdays became available and I've been doing them ever since – that was in 1998. I also do the odd dep in Harrogate.

It is very enjoyable doing the Wednesday evenings. Over the years I have made a lot of friends who are regular customers and I meet a lot of international tourists, especially from the USA and Canada. Downstairs, which was the bar in the 50s, there is a mirror which is covered with scratched signatures of servicemen who, just as we did in our time, used to meet there during World War Two, and we get lots of relatives of these people coming to see where their grandfathers or uncles met their friends while they were away from home during their time in the services.

One evening I was playing when one of the waitresses brought me a note from a young man who was sitting at a table and in it was a five pound note, and the message said: - "My grandfather was stationed in York during the war and told me that if ever I came, I should visit Betty's, buy the pianist a drink, and ask him to play *A Nightingale Sang in Berkeley Square*, so would you please play it for my granddad? And cheers!" The young man was from Canada.

Another nice thing happened in early 2003. One Wednesday evening I had been playing as usual and at about ten minutes to seven a lady, who had been sitting at a table on her own, came over and said she was enjoying my playing and did I just play here or did I play anywhere else, I told her that I played anywhere; she said how far would I travel, and I said Sydney, and have! Her name was Ann, and she told me she lived in Oxford but also had a home in South Western France where she planned to have a birthday party in the coming September and would I be prepared to play for her? I said I would be most pleased, and come September I went to France and played at her party. It was a wonderful three days and I was made most welcome and treated as a long time friend. They enjoyed it so much that it was repeated for her husband Peter's birthday the following year. It so happened that Peter was originally from Leeds and his cousin Stanley, who was at the party, is now a good friend and we often play the odd game of golf together.

In between the Betty's gig I have always been able to put in deps if something came along. I have put the occasional big band together to play for my friend, the impressionist Johnny More, who does a marvellous job on the Sinatra stuff, and Patti and I have done a lot of work for Warner's Holidays, but not anymore. It isn't worth it. The pay was ok for working Knaresborough but it wasn't enough to have to go to the Isle of Wight for the same money. We did quite a bit of work for Tony Peers, a former comic but now an agent/producer, who was the booker for the Grand Hotel chain, and we did two summer seasons for him in Scarborough, the last being at the Spa Theatre. I like Tony; he was always very fair with us.

Unfortunately the season at the Spa in 2002 was our last, because after working at the Grand Hotel, Scarborough on Saturday 28th February 2001, Patti could not get out of bed on the following Sunday morning and was diagnosed with rheumatoid arthritis. By the time we had come to the end of the '02 season it had become a lot worse and she had to stop performing.

After suffering four and a half years of pain I am happy to say she is now on a new wonder drug and is finding life a lot easier. The new anti TNF treatment started a month before our Silver

Wedding, for which we went to Rome, and as someone who struggled to walk a hundred yards before the treatment it was just amazing that one day she walked more than six miles between the Vatican, the Colisseum, the Trevi Fountain and the Spanish Steps.

For someone who has been performing since she was three years old you can imagine how hard it must be to have to stop. I am so proud of her because instead of feeling sorry for herself and crumbling into the "why me?" syndrome, she has re-invented herself and now teaches ICT for the Leeds College of Technology.

I book the acts for the regular monthly cabarets that we put on at our golf club, Howley Hall, and Patti comperes the shows – once in showbiz, always in showbiz! Sadly, she can't play golf anymore; the start of this dreadful disease coincided with her being Lady Captain at the club and at the time she had a handicap of twelve, which is very good. Unfortunately, because she can no longer play, there are times when she misses it badly, but then she will become all philosophical and say that she is working so much she hasn't the time anyway, but I know that deep down she really does miss it.

When I look back I realise what a wonderful time I have had making a living out of what is most people's hobby. It has enabled me to work with some of the best performers and musicians in the business, in some of the best venues, and given me the opportunity to travel the world.

For someone who never passed his eleven plus and never went to college or took a music exam I think I have done all right for myself. I know that anyone can achieve their ambitions if they are determined to work hard and take all the opportunities that come along, yes, sometimes you need a bit of luck, but I believe that if you put yourself into certain situations, luck will often come along. As the New York cop said to the little old lady who asked "how do you get to Carnegie Hall?" "PRACTICE MADAM, PRACTICE!"

My favourite theatre to work is the Blackpool Opera House, although the London Palladium was pretty special, and some of the concert halls including the Royal Concert Hall in Nottingham and the Fairfield Hall in Croydon were great, but one that stands out is the Waterfront Hall in Belfast which, acoustically, was just about perfect.

My favourite cities are Sydney and San Francisco but I have had wonderful times in Hong Kong, Dubai, Venice and Rome. I also enjoyed the times I spent in the Caribbean.

The Celebrity Golf Tour gave me the chance to play with not only my fellow entertainers but a lot of the sports stars I have followed and admired over the years and have become friends with.

I think fate has played a large part in my life. I was lucky to get into the band as a national serviceman: Batley Variety Club introduced me to the higher echelons of show business: The Dorothy Solomon Agency and the Bachelors opened a lot of doors for me: Jeanette Peters and the Harold Fielding office furthered my career and Bernard Hinchcliffe, Derek Franks, Lee James and Don Jones put a lot of work my way – even at this stage, those bloody song titles still keep cropping up!

If I could change anything at all it would be that this dreadful disease, rheumatoid arthritis, had not hit my wife Patti. But, all in all life has been good to me; I still play golf at Howley Hall Golf

Club with my regular four ball friends, Brian, John, and Bob - who describes us as "Three past captains and a top musician" – I think he means me! I still have my Betty's gigs, and I wouldn't rule out putting a big band together again sometime in the future. So you see, whether it is playing music with my musician friends or golf with my showbiz friends, I'm still *"Swingin' with the Stars"*!

This is a list of a lot of the people I have played trombone, piano, arranged or conducted for:-

Shirley Bassey, Freddie Starr, Johnny Mathis, Gracie Fields, Vince Hill, Tony Orlando, Vera Lynn, Tony Christie, Neil Sedaka, Vicki Carr, Stuart Damon, Kathy Kirby, Freda Payne, Salina Jones, Morecambe and Wise, Cilla Black, Norman Wisdom, The Drifters, Clodagh Rogers, Tommy Cooper, The Stylistics, Sandy Shaw, The Bachelors, The Supremes, Lulu, Freddie Davies, The Three Degrees, Olivia Newton John, Lena Zavaroni, Tony Darrel, Dusty Springfield, Neal Reed, Lovelace Watkins, Cleo Lain, Johnnie Dankworth, Tom Jones, Eartha Kitt, Moira Anderson, Dave Allen, Denise Nolan, The Nolan Sisters, Al Martino, Bob Monkhouse, Maggie Moon, Cliff Richard, Bernard Manning, Harry Secombe, Jimmy Edwards, Charlie Williams, Little Foxes, Michael Bentine, Jim Bowen, The Vernon Girls, Jimmy Tarbuck, Ken Goodwin, Cool Breeze, Kenny Lynch, Patti Gold, Dougie Brown, Guys and Dolls, Ray Allen, Lynn Perrie, Brotherhood of Man, Roy Walker, Bernie Clifton, The Hollies, Tom O Connor, Stutz Bear Cats, Roy Orbison, Buddy Greco, Wall Street Crash, Gene Pitney, Tommy Steel, Dallas Boys, Bobby Vee, Michael Crawford, Daly and Wayne, Bobby Rydell, Mike and Bernie Winters, Jerry Stevens, Frankie Lane, Jess Conrad, Lionel Blair, Guy Mitchell, Marty Wild, Billy Dainty, Joan Regan, Dickie Valentine, Ted Rogers, Ronnie Hilton, Ron Dale, Tony Monopoly, Mike Newman, Matt Monro, Max Bygraves, Michael Barrymore, Bruce Forsyth, Paul Daniels, Lennie Bennett, Jerry Munro, Peters and Lee, Benny York, Steve Montgomery, Lynn Paul, Josef Locke, The Grumbleweeds, Mike Burton, Ken Platt, Stu Francis, Janet Brown, Little and Large,

Robert Earl, The Krankies, Johnny Casson, Sheila Buxton, Terry Hall, Reginald Dixon, Dukes and Lee, Leslie Crowther, Mike Reed, Johnny Hackett, Walter Landaur, Liz Dawn, Gladys Mills, Paul Shane, Frankie Vaughan, Mike Terry, Les Dennis, Ken Dodd, Susan Maughan, Dustin Gee, Frank Carson, Anita Harris, Grace Kennedy, Norman Collier, Edwin Heath, Iris Williams, Lennie Henry, Lambert and Ross, Les Dawson, Frank Ifield, Lester and Smart, Bobby Crush, P.J. Proby, The Seekers, The New Seekers, Garry Lovini, Marti Caine, Joe Longthorn, Black and White Minstrels, David Copperfield, John Rowles, Donald Peers, Rod Hull, Peter Gordeno, Georgie Fame, Adam Faith, Joan Turner, Arthur Askey, Craig Douglas, Carl Wayne, Dorothy Squires, Johnny More, Jimmy Cricket, Pat O Hare, Lance Percival, Eli Woods, Aiden J Harvey, Ray Fell, Roger DeCourcey, Des O'Connor, Dean Raymond, Neville King, Martin St.James, Jeff Hooper, Millican and Nesbitt, Paul Squire, Bobby Knutt, Johnny Ray, Larry Grayson, Bobby Bennett, Al Read, Larry Parker, Tammy Jones, The Beverley Sisters, Black Abbots, Peter Goodright, Max Wall, Stan Boardman. Ivor Emmanuel, Jack Douglas, Judith Durham, Robert Young, Tony Hatch and Jackie Trent, Dana, Bill Tarmey, David Whitfield, Wayne King, James Casey, Winifred Attwell, Joe Church, Jimmy Edwards, Johnny Stafford, Jimmy Ruffin, Gordon Peters, Bill Martin, Gerard Kenny, Dudley Doolittle, Mike Yarwood, Maxine Barry, Bobby Pattinson, Clive Webb, Tommy Bruce, Rocking Berries, Dawson Chance, Alan Stewart, Terry Webster, Ward Allan, George Holmes, Tony Dowling, Clark Brothers, Dave Evans, Stella Starr, Tiny Tim, Val Doonican, Ruby Murray, Cannon and Ball, Barbara Law, Frances Yip, Bob Carolgees, Wayne Dobson, Billy Pearce, Will Gains, Ray Martine,

Tony Selby, Jerry Harris, Lori Wells, Wee Willie Harris, Hughie Green, John Bouchire, Des King, Monica Rose, John Paul Jones, Tony Adams, Derek Dene, Nicky Martin, Hope and Keen, Paul Melba, Paul Boardman, Danny Roman, Max Peters, Gale West, George Hamilton IV , Joanne Shields, Tommy Sutton, Everly Bros., Joe Brown, Anne Shelton, Stan Richards, Rosemary Squires, Brian Marshall, Mike Lancaster, Morgan Lee James, Sid Francis, Judy Moxon, Jonathan Lavelle, Jimmy Marshal, Dai Francis, Tony Peers, Jane Beaumont, Linda Newport, Arthur Worsley, The Spinners, The Squadronairs Orchestra, BBC Scottish Orchestra, BBC NDO, Arthur Greenslade, Roy Castle, Reflections, Chick Murray, Johnny Hawkins, John Barry, Geoff Love, Stan Reynolds, Johnny Pearson, Johnny Spence, Roy Rogasin, Brian Fahay, Yorkshire Television, BBC Radio Leeds, Channel 7 (Australia), NFK (Tokyo), Yamaha Festival Orchestra (Tokyo), Orchestra de Mexico, Orchestra of the Czech TV System, Yorkshire Imperial Metals Brass Band, Derek Franks Organization, Cunard, Harold Fielding Ltd., The Delfont Organization, MAM, McLeod Holden, P&O Cruises, Tony Peers Productions, Lee James Agency, Bernard Hinchcliffe Productions - - - - and these are just the ones I remember!

Here are some of the countries I've been to:-

Abu Dhabi, Alaska, Antigua, Aruba, Ascension Isles, Barbados, Bahrain, Belgium, Bonaire, Borneo, Brunei, Bulgaria, Canada, Canary Isles, Cayman Isles, Cape Verde, Czechoslovakia, Colombia, Costa Rica, Corfu, Corsica, Crete, Curacao, Cyprus, Denmark, Dominica, Dubai, Egypt, Elba, Falklands, Fiji, Finland, France, Gambia, Georgia, Germany, Grenada, Greece, Gozo, Guernsey, Hawaii, Holland, Hong Kong, India, Ireland, Isle of Man, Isle of Wight, Israel, Italy, Jamaica, Japan, Jersey, Jordan, Kenya, Kos, Key West, Madeira, Majorca, Malaya, Malta, Maui, Mikinos, Morocco, Mayrou, Mexico, Minorca, Norway, New Zealand, Oman, Pakistan, Panama, Poland, Portugal, Puerto Rico, Qatar, Russia, Rhodes, Santorini, Sardinia, Scotland, Sicily, Sierra Leone, Senegal, Sharjah, Singapore, Seychelles, Spain, South Africa, St Lucia, St Kitts, Sweden, Syria, Tahiti, Thailand, Tortola, Tobago Tunisia, Turkey, Ukraine, U.S.A., Vietnam, Venezuela, Wales, Western Samoa, Yugoslavia and Zakinthos.